PAGES OF PASSION BOOK 3: RISING WAVES

AN AUTOBIOGRAPHY

GEORGE HATCHER

Previously published as Billion Dollar Rainmaker Part I in 2021

This book can be purchased at over 40,000 bookstores and libraries, including brick-and-mortar stores, online, in print and digital, including Apple, Kindle, and Audible formats. Casa Hatcher Press books are available at special quantity discounts for bulk purchases, sales promotions, premiums, and educational use for fundraising. Casa Hatcher Press is a subsidiary of Pretty Face, Inc., Rancho Mirage, California 92270.

For details, contact:

Casa Hatcher Press. http://casahatcherpress.com (800) 416-6189

Copyright © 2025 by George Hatcher. All rights reserved. Printed in the United States of America and abroad.

No part of this book may be used in any manner except in the case of brief quotations in critical articles or reviews.

Book and cover designed by Casa Hatcher Press

Pages of Passion Book 3: Rising Waves, by George J. Hatcher

Revision: 04-10-2025

LCCN: 2024951928

ISBN: 979-8-9919018-2-6 (Hardcover)

ISBN: 979-8-9882886-7-1 (Paperback)

ISBN: 979-8-9919018-3-3 (EPUB)

DEDICATION

Molly,

In the beautiful choreography of life, you are my steadfast partner, bringing cherished harmony to every moment we share.

With all my love,

George

INTRODUCTION

RERUN

Marriage and Disillusionment

At seventeen, I married Selena while serving in the Navy—a decision that felt thrilling at the moment. In a reckless burst of passion, I went AWOL and fled to her hometown in Mexico, where I opened an ice cream parlor in her old neighborhood, dreaming of a fresh start. But the exhilaration didn't last long; soon, my past caught up with me. The FBI tracked me down, delivering a harsh warning: they'd be back if I didn't turn myself in before I turned eighteen.

Just days before my eighteenth birthday, I discovered that Selena was having an affair with her former fiancé—the one she had sworn she was finished with. That revelation shattered our marriage.

A Desperate Escape

One late evening, my wife's sister drove me across the border from Mexico, with me hidden in the trunk of the car. Fear gripped me at every rumble of the tires on the pavement, especially for her safety. As we approached the crossing, I wrestled with the decision to turn myself in to the Navy, which I wanted to do. I believed that surrendering would be the better choice, possibly earning some leniency with the judge since I was returning on my own. However, the thought of being arrested loomed over me like a dark cloud, filling me with dread. I couldn't shake the feeling that being caught would lead to a far worse outcome than the self-surrender I was seeking.

Somehow, I made it across to El Paso and caught a train to Los Angeles. Yet, my destination for surrender was San Diego—the last place I had been stationed before going AWOL. Upon arrival, however, I hesitated, caught between fear and the desire to make things right. Instead, I found myself behind bars in a Tijuana jail, where I practically begged the shore patrol to arrest me and bring me back to the USA. The conditions in that jail were horrendous.

Facing the Consequences

I was sent to a Marine brig, serving a four-month sentence that was intense, to say the least. Even amidst the struggle, I knew I deserved it. Upon my release, I was supposed to return to the Navy to complete my four-year term, but fate had other plans. Just as I stepped out of the brig, detectives from Los Angeles arrested me on a charge of grand theft.

The allegation? Borrowing $3,500 from my girlfriend's mother under false pretenses when I was around fifteen years old. It felt surreal as the judge, in that case, sentenced me to the California

Youth Authority and sent me to DVI, Deuel Vocational Institution—a place I insist is a prison, far from anything resembling juvenile hall. In total, I spent about 27 months incarcerated, locked away as my past decisions haunted me.

A New Beginning

Upon release on parole for a year, I found a job as a janitor at a downtown Los Angeles department store just two days later. It was there that I met Alicia, who had an apartment with Clara. Together, we engaged in something crooked that would later be referred to as the "locker thing."

Eventually, a fantastic opportunity knocked on my door: an apprenticeship in Air Conditioning and Heating, which made me a union member. The pay was significantly better than my janitor job, but my personal life remained tumultuous. After more than a year of dating, Alicia became my second wife, but our marriage lasted only 24 days before we divorced.

Building a Business Amidst Chaos

Living with my parents was meant to be temporary—a pause until I could afford something nicer for myself and my second wife. After the quick divorce, I moved into an apartment in Monterey Park, California, where I met Ava and Emma, two call girls living next door. We quickly became friends, but my life continued to swirl in chaos.

Not long after, I was presented with an opportunity to buy a body, fender, and paint business in East Los Angeles. It was a sizable shop, brimming with potential. However, I lacked the necessary capital; it was still too early in my life to have saved much. Despite this, I boldly quit my job and purchased the business.

Cash Flow Challenges

My personal life took another turn when I married for the third time to Sophia, who gave birth to my daughter, Judy. The business I purchased quickly became my cash cow, producing over ten car paint jobs daily and bodywork. I eventually expanded to include a mechanic and a car upholstery department, taking on numerous collision jobs authorized by insurance companies.

Yet, with success came significant challenges. I had to front the costs for repairs, and once jobs were completed, I often waited weeks or even months for payments from the insurance companies. This created serious cash flow issues, especially when I needed to pay bills at the end of the month.

Pages of Passion Book 3: Rising Waves begins here.

PICTURES IN THIS BOOK

Dear Reader,

As you embark on this journey through my life, I want to share a unique aspect of this autobiography. Alongside my words, you will find a handful of selected images that complement my stories and memories. While these photos are not direct representations of the individuals I've written about, they serve to illustrate and evoke the essence of my experiences. For instance, a friend is referred to as Elena in this narrative, but it's important to note that "Elena" is not her real name, and the AI-generated image representing her does not depict her alone; it captures the essence of a character playing the part of Elena in my book.

In reflecting on my life, I've included images of significant people, places, and moments that shaped who I am today. From a stock photo of a child delivering canned food—reminiscent of my industrious youth when I sold canned goods I received from my father—to a vibrant portrayal of lettuce in the fields, reminding me of the days my dad took me to the lettuce fields, where workers picked lettuce and loaded his truck with crates of it, these visuals add another layer to my narrative.

Additionally, I've illustrated elements of my father's business, particularly a striking image of garlic, which represents the hard work and dedication that defined his life. These images are not just decorative; they are meant to enhance your understanding and connection to the stories I share.

Thank you for joining me on this personal journey. I hope these images enrich your reading experience and allow you to visualize my memories as vividly as I have.

WARNING!

Adult matter

This book is designed for an adult audience. It contains themes of violence and sexual behavior that are not suitable for minors, sensitive readers, or individuals living in the current chaotic world, where incurable sexually transmitted diseases and a pandemic have confined us to solitary spaces within our homes. While my life is not a work of fiction, the names of some individuals I have encountered have been altered to preserve their privacy.

All of the characters, organizations, and events depicted in this novel have likely been shaped by the passage of time, forgetfulness, and a timeline that was adjusted for the sake of expediency.

ALSO BY GEORGE HATCHER

Mario 1: Woman in Jeopardy

Mario 2: Coming of Age

Mario 3: Risky Business

Mario 4: Free Fall

Mario 5: Afire

Mario 6: Marked

Mario 7: Aftershock

Mario 8: Captivated

Single Titles

One Wilshire

Gabi

Rico

Cats: Meow Is The Language Of Love

HER: Artistic Expressions Through AI

Elegance In White: Through Wedding Gowns

Quinceañera Fashion: Fifteen & Fabulous

Billion Dollar Rainmaker Part I

Pages of Passion Book 1: My First 19 Years

Pages of Passion Book 2: Bold Beginnings

COMING SOON

Pages of Passion Book 4: Threads Of Destiny

Pages of Passion Book 5

Pages of Passion Book 6

Pages of Passion Book 7

Mario 9

Gabi 2

Rico 2

1

CHESTER

I was doing estimates one morning, and Chester was one of our customers. He brought his car for an estimate on bodywork and a paint job. He wanted something better than the thirty-five-dollar option.

He was the manager of PetroMe, a large gas station located half a block away on Brooklyn Avenue, on our side of the street. I often walked past his station to get to either [1]Donald's or [2] Carlos's office. PetroMe was a local chain with twice as many pumps as the big-name stations. PetroMe operated over eighty stations throughout Los Angeles County.

"I cash some of your employee paychecks," he said. "Been meaning to come over to say hi, but this place is always mobbed, and your parking lot is bumper to bumper."

Chester was thirty-two and drove a sporty Plymouth with beautiful chrome wheels.

---

1. Donald was my accountant
2. Carlos was my attorney

"You have a good-looking lacquer paint job on this car," I said. "Why paint unless you are looking for a different color?"

"That's exactly what I want. I want a midnight blue metallic lacquer."

"Chester, that will take over a week to do. Even if I give you a break, it will set you back seven hundred big ones."[3]

"How about the bodywork?"

"I'll throw that in," I said.

"Do it," he said.

Luis had just finished painting a car. He came out with his mask on. I introduced them.

"He wants a lacquer job, midnight blue metallic."

Luis turned all smiles. "I do a terrific job. It will look fantastic!"

Chester shook his hand. "Here are the keys, Luis. I've seen you over at the station. Let me know when it's ready."

It was our first complete lacquer paint job. We did a lot of spot-painting with lacquer, but not the whole car.

"He's the manager at PetroMe," Luis said after Chester left. "Lines of people cash their checks there."

I was lucky to have Luis. Every car he painted was perfect. I'd never seen a run on any job he ever did. When painting with enamel, like we did the thirty-five-dollar jobs, a run in the paint would not be unexpected, but the painter can fix it quickly. How do I know? I learned a lot in that business.

---

3. Adjusted for inflation, $700.00 in 1962 is equal to $5,996.06 in 2020.

I was fortunate that several insurance companies encouraged their clients who lived in our area and were involved in accidents to have repairs done at my shop. However, once I completed a job, it often took a month or more to receive payment. Farmers Insurance was the exception; their clients received checks made out to both them and my auto center, allowing us to get paid upon the delivery of the car.

Handling insurance collision work requires fronting the costs of labor, parts, and materials, which strained my cash flow, especially given the volume of work I had. While cash payments for paint and minor bodywork helped alleviate some of this cash flow issue, it wasn't a complete solution.

When I was seventeen, I married Selena, and we honeymooned in Mexico. However, that trip took an unexpected turn when I ended up AWOL (Absent Without Leave) from the Navy in Juarez, where I decided to open an ice cream parlor and figured I could forgo returning.

I didn't honeymoon in Mexico when I married my second wife, Alicia, but I did when I married my third wife, Sophia. I had a deep love for Mexico—perhaps the freedom I felt at that age drew me to it. There was so much to explore.

It had been a long time since Ramirez[4] left, and I felt it was time for a break. I wanted to revisit Mexico, this time with Elena, my girlfriend. I was grateful to have her by my side, working and living with me. We worked endless hours and needed a break.

"Let's go to Acapulco," I suggested.

---

4. Ramirez sold me the Auto Body & Paint shop.

"How can we both go?" she asked.

"Gil and Mike can handle it. We'll give them keys and let them take care of things. If they can't manage it by now, then they shouldn't be working here."

The look on Elena's face was worth the cost of ten trips.

I DIDN'T WANT to leave the shop short of cash. Don was scheduled to come in and do the payroll on the weekend I was going to miss, but I wanted to be sure that Mike and Gil had cash if we ran out of supplies from a vendor who didn't give us credit.

Chester was a happy camper with the work on his car. To save a trip to the bank, I went to him to cash the check that would give the shop a safety net while I was gone, plus help cover the trip expenses. I told him about our upcoming trip to Mexico. Twenty-five thousand pesos in Mexico would go a long way; even at the Hilton, the daily rate was fifty US dollars.[5] That was a beachside room.

"Is it okay if I make it two thousand?" I asked Chester.
"Make it any amount you want," he said.
"Two is good."
"Want me to hold it or put it through?"
I wish he had never asked me that.

---

5. Adjusted for inflation, $50.00 in 1962 is equal to $428.29 in 2020.

"What do you mean?"

Chester chuckled. "I can deposit it when you get back. No sweat."

"Thanks," I said. "You can deposit now. It's good."

He counted out the money.

"You didn't take the fee," I said.

"Enjoy Mexico, my friend. Don't sweat the fee. It's a pleasure."

"Chester, you're a trooper. Thanks."

Chester's domain was nestled behind the thick, impenetrable glass of a small cubicle—a stronghold designed to be both break-in-proof and, I imagined, bulletproof, safeguarding him and the cash he handled daily. From his secure perch, he offered me a casual wave, his familiar gesture breaking through the sterile barrier of the teller window where he sat diligently cashing checks. I waved back.

2

ACAPULCO

We took a taxi to the airport, checked in, and passed through customs. The roundtrip to Acapulco for both of us cost a hundred and fifty dollars. Making our way to the gate, we entered a fenced-off area bustling with well-dressed travelers, much like ourselves, blending office wear with Sunday best.

In the lounge, we settled into seats by the window, where we could see our plane waiting. I watched as various crews busied themselves with pre-flight tasks. Elena leaned toward the window, her legs crossed, accentuating the vibrant colors of her pastel miniskirt and clunky heels. While my black button-down shirt and matching khakis weren't as comfortable as jeans, I had plenty of jeans, swim trunks, and shorts packed in my suitcase for our trip.

"This is exciting," I said.

"I always get excited before a trip," Elena said. "You've never asked me about the gap between when I graduated from high school and when I came looking for a job at the shop."

"If you want me to know, you'll tell me, like you told me

about your brother putting you into a casket. What other surprises are you hiding in there?" I squinted at her as if I could see straight inside her brain.

Elena laughed.

"After I graduated, I flew to Hawaii by myself. My aunt thought I was going with friends, and I would have, but none of my friends who were up to Hawaii could afford it. I was supposed to be gone for a week but stayed for six months. I told my aunt that I met a rich man who owned a big house and that he offered to let me stay there as a caretaker to babysit the house when he was away from Hawaii."

"Was it true?"

"Kind of. My aunt wasn't happy about it. I gave her the house number and told her to call me anytime. She never called me once. I called her about once a week. She stopped asking me when I was coming back about a month after I got to Hawaii. I think she was glad I was out of her hair."

I stared at her for a second. "What exactly does 'kind of true' mean?"

The activity behind the gate's desk increased, and a uniformed man opened the door leading to the plane. He called for first class to begin boarding, so we got up and boarded first. On the plane, we were offered champagne, wine, and refreshments. We wanted CC water and got Seagram's Seven Water. We sipped and drank slowly. They are supposed to taste the same because they are both Bourbons. Don't believe it. When the plane was lifting off, we were checking out the menu. Once we were in flight, a movie appeared on a screen ahead of us: *The Birds*. Then we were in Acapulco, in a taxi, and finally at the hotel. Our room was stellar. While it was daylight, we hit the beach, then ordered in and ate fish tacos in the room.

Elena was eating away.

"So, where were we?" I scratched my head like I was thinking about it. "What exactly does 'kind of true' mean?"

For half a second, Elena had a blank look, then she laughed.

"I am in Hawaii, walking along a busy street. A convertible Rolls Royce passes by, and I see the brake lights. The driver gets out of the car. His car is blocking his lane. Cars are screeching around the Rolls; there's honking and chaos. He walks towards me with his hand out. 'My name is David Marks. Can I give you a lift?' He was fifty-something, or older or younger. I didn't ask his age."

"You're making this up," I said with a grin.

In Acapulco, we found ourselves immersed in endless conversation.

We escaped to a fabulous restaurant, its tall, pitched roof crafted from vibrant palapas, where the atmosphere was a refreshing departure from our usual concerns.

I reveled in the restaurant's open-air ambiance, surrounded by lush gardens that enhanced our dining experience. The air was rich with the enticing scents of chili, cumin, and a medley of spices, intermingled with the sweet fragrance of ripe fruit and the refreshing breezes wafting in from the beach. Being there with Elena made it all the more special as we savored every bite and each other's company, the worries of the shop fading into a distant memory.

"When you came to Acapulco before, did you fly?" Elena asked, sipping a tall fruit drink with the required umbrella.

"Yes, Sophia and I flew. Sophia was my third wife. Selena, my first wife, and I traveled to Mexico City in a car and then drove to Guadalajara, and we headed back to her home, Juarez, a border city of El Paso, Texas.

"Damn, that must have taken days and days."

"It took days, right!"

The waitress delivered our food. We'd both ordered delicious and surprisingly inexpensive seafood grilled with a Mexican flair.

No matter where we went, no matter what Elena wore, men rubbernecked and gaped at her. I noticed it when we walked in and out of restaurants, at touristy hot spots, shops, and, of course, at the beach. They flirted with her, and she flirted right back. In the restaurant, a guy with his date walked by and gave Elena the once over. She winked at me and gave him the once-over right back at him.

"Hey, you don't do that back home," I teased.

"We're on vacation. I feel so free here in Mexico like we can do anything. I like to flirt, and I know you don't care." She flashed me the biggest of smiles. "Tell me it bugs you, baby, and I'll stop."

"I can't blame them," I said. "How can I blame them? How could they resist?"

"Tell me you love my ass," she said.

"I do love your ass," I said. "When we are back in the room, I will tear your bathing suit off. I'm going to bite your ass cheeks and tongue you until you scream with pleasure."

She told the waitress approaching us, [1]"*Apurate, vamos ir a cojer en el cuarto.*"

The waitress handed me the tab and a pen and said, [2]"*Que linda pareja son ustedes.*"

We were lying in bed in heat once we were back in the room.

It was the other kind of heat.

Elena said, "You never fucked me there? How come?"

"I waited until we came to Mexico, where we're free to do anything."

"G, do it, but don't hurt me."

"I would never hurt you."

"Hurry."

Our room was in the same hotel where I had stayed with Sophia. Elena never asked where I stayed before, so it never came up. I never asked her what hotel she stayed in before David Marks took her home with him.

---

1. Hurry up already we're going to the room to fuck.
2. What a beautiful couple you are.

When Elena showed me six bathing suits, it reminded me of when Sophia showed me what she brought. Elena's assortment was striking. All of them showed lots of skin.

"I'll wear whatever you want me to wear," she said, posing in the striking white and blue bikini.

"I like what you have on," I said. "Let's hit the beach."

We didn't stop with that. We went out clubbing. What we called strip shows in the USA was no comparison to those all over Acapulco. One reminded me of the girl who took a bath on stage in Ensenada when I was with Alicia, my third wife, but compared to what we saw in Acapulco, Ensenada was tame.

IN OUR COZY hotel room in Acapulco, the vibrant sounds of the beach filtered through the slightly open window. I found myself calling Mike every day, anxious to hear about the business back home. This was a time before cell phones, when every international call felt like a luxury, costing far more than I cared to admit.

"Stop calling," Mike shouted, his voice straining to cut through the clamor of the shop behind him. "Enjoy yourself! I've got everything under control. You need to stop worrying!"

I couldn't help but also reach out to Sophia, wanting to check on her and our daughter, Judy. Each conversation brought a mix of relief and worry, tethering me to responsibilities I was trying to escape.

"What can I do to help you relax?" Elena asked, her voice soft yet playful, breaking through my spiraling thoughts.

"I'm relaxed—totally," I replied, mustering a smile though my fingers still itched for the phone.

"Then stop using it," she suggested, a teasing lilt in her voice.

"You're right," I conceded. "Okay. Okay. No more phone calls."

With that, Elena spread her arms wide, inviting me into her embrace. I stepped into her warmth, and we hugged, lost in the moment. Our mouths met in a passionate kiss, and the world outside faded away, leaving only us and the electric chemistry that crackled in the air.

Elena and I took in the sights, our eyes drawn to the breathtaking views of the Acapulco coastline. The sun glistened on the azure waters, and the sound of crashing waves filled the air, adding to the vibrant atmosphere. As we strolled along the cliffside at La Quebrada, we watched in awe as the daring divers prepared to leap off the towering rocks, their silhouettes framed against the sky.

With skillful grace, they ascended to the edge, where the world below seemed to fade away. Then, in an exhilarating moment, they launched themselves into the air, arms outstretched, plunging into the ocean with a splash that sent up a shower of droplets catching the sunlight. The crowd gathered at the bottom erupted in cheers and applause, captivated by their bravery and precision.

Elena squeezed my hand, excitement sparkling in her eyes. "Can you believe how fearless they are?" she exclaimed, and I nodded, mesmerized by the scene unfolding before us. At that moment, we both felt a surge of adrenaline, vicariously sharing in the adrenaline-fueled thrill of the divers as they danced between earth and sea, embodying the spirit of adventure that defined our time in Acapulco.

3

ACAPULCO BYE BYE

Before we knew it, we were back home. We arrived on a Wednesday afternoon, ordered two pizzas, and spent the rest of the day and night in bed. We took Thursday off to get over our vacation. Why did we come back from vacation tired? Take a wild guess.

THEN, it was Friday, time to return to the daily grind. Elena stretched her arm out as I drove in and played with my hair. It was short and curly, and nothing ever messed it up, but she liked trying.

"I feel closer to you," she said. "Thank you for the lovely trip."

"I dug it too," I said, caressing her face.

Less than ten minutes after our arrival we had a customer who wanted a paint job or something done to their car.

"You can't carry thirty thousand dollars in receivables," Don said during his regular work visit. "This is ludicrous."

I wasn't in the mood for our regular exchanges. Going cold turkey from the vacation to the shop, I wasn't full of answers. I had no solution to throw at him as I usually did.

Don glanced over at me from his seat at my desk, his expression serious. "You don't have enough in the bank to cover the supply bills. You're stocking up on new parts and supplies for the insurance work like never before."

I sat on the sofa opposite the desk, the blinds partially closed, though they did little to muffle the vibrant sounds of the bustling shop below. I could hear the steady hum of the compressor and the rhythmic clinking of metal tools in use.

"That's because the insurance jobs are focused on newer cars," I explained. "Customers won't settle for used parts—after all, they're only paying a deductible, and the insurance foots the rest of the bill. Even if we source used parts, they don't save us much. The junk car market is just wild these days."

Don nodded, his brow furrowed with concern. "I've seen it happen to other shops I work with - they damaged their credit, and now they're forced to deal with suppliers on a cash-only basis. I'd hate for that to happen to you."

"Write all the checks that must be written and leave them on my desk, ready to mail. Before you leave, tell me how much I need to deposit to clear them."

"I'll do that, sure. You can hold my check. No rush on that."

"Nonsense," I said. "Write your check as you always do and use it. It's not like I don't have any money in the bank."

Donald wrote twelve thousand one hundred dollars in checks. For all of them to clear, I needed to deposit six thousand two hundred dollars. The solution would be to collect from the damn insurance carriers that took so long to pay me after their insureds got their cars back.

I CALLED Chester at the gas station.

"Do you have five or ten minutes to chat if I come over?"

"You don't need an appointment," he laughed. "I'm here."

4

NOTHING IS FREE

As I pulled into the PetroMe station, the fading evening light cast a warm orange glow over the empty pumps. The only sound was the soft hum of the fluorescent lights above, starkly contrasting with the usual bustle of activity that filled the air during peak hours. I shut off the engine and stepped out into the crisp evening air; my eyes scanned the doors as I made my way inside. I was immediately greeted by the familiar sight of rows of snacks and drinks lining the shelves.

I approached the cashier's station, where a thick wall of glass separated me from Chester, who regarded me with a mix of curiosity and familiarity. I waved, and he nodded before disappearing. Moments later, he emerged from behind the bulletproof enclosure, his expression softening into a friendly smile.

"What a surprise to see you! How was your trip to Mexico?" he asked.

"It was great! But I returned to a cash flow crisis," I chuckled. "I should have extended my vacation."

Chester laughed. "Can I help?"

"I need $7,000 to meet upcoming supplier payments. My accounts receivable from insurance companies for repairs on insured vehicles are kicking my ass. The delays in receiving payments after completing the jobs seem like an eternity. Business is great, but the cash flow is a bitch."

"Sounds like you need me to cash a seven-thousand-dollar

check and not deposit your check until you have the money in the bank."

"If you can't do it. It's great. No pressure."

"I can do it. Let me explain how check cashing works here. The owners profit from cashing checks," he said, "but our main goal is selling gas. Offering check-cashing services attracts customers all week." He leaned in slightly, adopting a more conversational tone. "I keep a good amount of cash on hand to manage operations. Today's checks will be deposited, and I'll have cash that cash available tomorrow. We charge a transaction fee. Cashing $7,000 in smaller checks would bring in about $40 in fees, not to mention the profit from gas sales."

"How much will it cost me to get seven thousand and hold the check for five days?"

A guy came in the door with a leather jacket and a cigarette hanging out of his mouth. The ancient clunker he was driving looked like it used more oil than gas, and it turned out that he had come in to buy oil for his car. Chester returned to his iron room and handled the customer. After the guy drove off with a case of oil, leaving a thick black exhaust trail, Chester came back with a proposal for me.

"Write four checks to yourself that add up to seven thousand, endorse them, and I can hold them for a week before depositing. It'll cost you $100 to make this happen. Does that work for you?"

"That works," I said with lots of relief.

"I'll call you before I deposit the checks," he said.

"Great," I said. "Thanks, Chester."

I WENT BACK to my office, wrote four checks to myself, endorsed them, took them to Chester, and he gave me the cash. In the morning, I deposited the seven thousand cash plus the daily deposit from the day before. At the post office, I dropped off the envelopes with checks that Donald had left me to mail.

I told Elena.

"You genius," she said, raising her palm to bump mine. "It was quite cool that you thought of Chester and got him to do it. All you need now are some drafts[1] from the fucking insurance to pay Chester."

"Right. In the meantime, it costs me $20[2] a day, a hundred bucks."

"I get it," she said. "You are taking seven thousand out of circulation for them to cash checks."

"You so smart," I said. "I didn't stop to figure that their cash box would be short seven thousand dollars to cash customer checks until I paid it back by having Chester deposit the checks."

"Exactly, baby."

"If my bank loaned me the money, I would be paying the bank interest. I don't know how it compares to what I have to pay Chester, but either way, nothing is free. A hundred for five days for seven thousand is not cheap."

"You needed the money."

"Now I got to pay it back."

She looked around to see who was listening. The shop was a hive of activity. Everyone was too busy to be paying attention to us. Luis had a car going that he was painting. Two maskers were on the next car. The sander was grinding away. Gil was talking to someone who just drove up, and Mike was handling a pick-up.

"Let's hit the office for a quickie," she offered.

I loved her sexy smile.

---

1. Drafts are checks
2. Adjusted for inflation, $20.00 in 1962 is equal to $171.32 in 2020.

We were up the stairs in under a minute and doing it a minute after locking the office door.

CALLING the insurance company to inquire about the drafts they owed me often expedited the payment process. Unfortunately, Farmers was still the only insurance carrier willing to make payments upon completion of the work. However, my persistent follow-ups helped speed up several checks, and I sent Elena to pick them up. The influx of that money and our regular deposits gave me just enough to cover what I owed Chester. Seven thousand dollars in the sixties was a whole lot of money.

"You can deposit the four checks," I said to Chester. "Anything you need, come over."

"George, the same goes here. If you need to do that again, it's no sweat. I trust you."

A couple of days later, Chester asked me if I had a connection with Goodyear Tires. His metallic blue Plymouth needed four. I made a call and had the tires delivered to my shop.

I called Chester.

"There's a catch," I said. "I don't have the equipment to install them, but the tires are here. Come get them."

"How much do I owe you?"

"One dollar," I said.

"Can I call you G?"

"Sure. Why not?"

"G, you the man."

"No, Chester, you the man."

I looked up from some paperwork I was filling out and who walked in, but Mauro, the life-saving electrician who had brought daylight into my junk bin of a shop, lighting its way to success. He had worked magic for me and the meat market, and I still felt grateful.

"Hey man," Mauro said.

I half-expected him to ask for a paint job for himself or the young man who had walked in with him. The very young man. He was tall and slim, and as we shook hands, I noticed his hands were calloused but clean.

"This is Jose," Mauro said.

"I'm a mechanic," Jose said in Spanish. "I don't have a green card, but I don't have a wife or kids either."

"No disrespect," I said. "You're very young to be very savvy. What kind of mechanic?"

"Jefe, in Mexico, I was under a car with my dad when I was seven years old. I can fix any car."

I looked from Jose to Mauro, who raised his eyebrows. I reached out and retook Jose's hand and looked at it. I saw traces of grease staining his cuticles and callouses, lending his expertise credence.

"He's from my town in Mexico. I knew his dad. May he rest in peace. I've seen Jose work."

I shook my head. "I can't afford another person on the payroll," I said.

Jose had a stubborn chin. His eyes locked on mine, earnest and determined. "Jefe find me a spot, like way over there," he pointed. "I can do brake jobs and anything else you want. We split the profit. If I have no work, I have no pay."

"Is that going to be enough to live on? How will you survive?"

"He's living with me," Mauro said.

"What about tools?"

"I have tools," Jose said.

We walked to the back of the shop. I pointed out two spots for mechanic work.

"Maybe here," I said.

"I will bring my tools tomorrow with your permission," Jose said. "I have everything. With two hundred, I can buy a hoist and some other big items I couldn't bring with me."

"You brought all your tools from Mexico? How?"

He didn't say. He just touched his index finger to his temple as a sign of being smart.

THE NEXT MORNING, when I unlocked the gate, Jose and Mauro were waiting in Jose's truck. He set up four stackable toolboxes that looked lovely in the back where nothing was going on.

My sign painter made a good-looking sign that said mechanic work, brake special, transmissions, and motor overhauls.

I came up with the two hundred dollars, and we were in business.

The first job was a customer in for a paint job who asked for a price on a tune-up and brakes. I turned him over to Jose.

It didn't take long for Jose to be busy.

Elena and I had lunch in the office and talked about the latest developments.

"He has the best disposition of anyone I know."

She nodded in agreement.

"That's a positive, G. Always a smile on his face."

"He's only 24," I said.

"I heard," Elena said. "He dwarfs Mauro. What is he? Six two? Six four?"

"That toolbox is six feet," I said. "He tops it by three inches, at least."

"Without Ramirez here, our team is the new generation," Elena said.

Joe was good-looking. It wouldn't take long for a woman to find him.

5

EASTLAND AUTO CENTER II

On my way to the bank, I noticed the corner of Whittier and Rowan was for lease. Like Brooklyn Avenue, where my shop was, Whittier was heavily trafficked. Rowan was the same cross street we were on. On my way back from the bank, I was still thinking about it. I told Elena about it.

"It's too small to do any work there. It's tiny. I can paint it up, put signs on it advertising this place, or I can put someone there to do estimates while we do the work here."

"Let's drive over and look."

We walked around the parking lot. It was small, but the traffic on Whittier was too heavy to count.

"If I put someone here, the corner will advertise for us. It's all about the signage."

Elena kissed me. "You the brains, daddy."

"Now it's daddy?'

"What do you want me to call you?"

I kissed her. "G sounds better than daddy."

"G it is!"

I rented the place for a hundred dollars, month to month [1] with no lease. The landlord agreed to let me paint it and put signs on it as long as I didn't break any sign laws. We set up samples of paint there and a place to wait if more than one person was waiting to talk to someone.

I called in the painter who had done Eastland and Mauro for the wiring.

"I want to keep the upgrade dirt cheap but looking great," I said. "I can't afford anything expensive."

The Eastland sign said, 'Insurance Estimates.'

Now that I owned two Eastland Auto Centers, I sent Gil to Whittier to write estimates after the place was spiffed up. From that location, I wanted more paint jobs, small bodywork, and mechanic work for Jose. It would have been enough with the advertising signs. I didn't need to have a human in attendance.

"There's no time to take a bathroom break. If Gil is going over there, we need a replacement here," Elena said.

"No time for other things, either," I said. "Let's look around. I like hiring referrals from people we know."

I hired Alexa as a part-time trainee.

I saw Mike looking her over and told him, "Yes, she's attractive, but she's not here to distract you. I want her to learn, not entertain you. Save it for your Vicki."

"I got plenty for all," he said. He wasn't joking or showing off. That was just his attitude. I had no complaints about Mike. He was a hard worker, and he showed up on time.

"If she can learn the basics, send her to Whittier Boulevard and bring back Gil," Elena said. "You don't even need anyone there."

---

1. Adjusted for inflation, $100.00 in 1962 is equal to $856.58 in 2020.

"I agree. I don't plan to have someone there all the time. I want to get a feel."

"Feel this," Elena said.

"You stay nasty."

"Yes," she replied.

OVER THE YEARS, I've identified two primary factors that can cripple a business: excessive payroll and high rent. In my situation, payroll was manageable, given the volume of work I handled, and my rent was practically negligible. I realized, however, that my real vulnerability lay in my commitment to insurance work. While those lucrative, high-paying jobs beckoned enticingly, I lacked the financial buffer to sustain myself during the wait for payment.

A MONTH LATER, I found myself reaching out to Chester. I borrowed $9,000 at a daily cost of $25. Over the course of ten days, I paid it all back, making regular deposits instead of waiting to settle everything at once. I handed him checks in exchange for the cash, all while waiting in his queue, observing a colorful mix of customers. There were spotless office workers, busy shop owners, frazzled housewives, and even some homeless drunks. Many of them were simply cashing checks, not buying gas for cars they didn't even own.

"Aren't you afraid they'll hold you up?" I asked him as I watched a guy in threadbare rags walk off toward a nearby liquor store while counting his cash.

"I'm more afraid of getting shot in the process. The money's not mine. That doesn't mean I'm giving it away. If someone goes for it, I'll shoot them with the shotgun we keep in the booth."

"Chester, you got balls."

"The office is solid steel. The window is bulletproof glass. I'm safer in the cube than out here."

"Let me know if you need anything," I said. "I feel bad coming to you like this and not giving you something back."

I handed him a fifty for himself. He took it with a big smile.

When I look back on the women I've written about, they were essentially my social circle back then. My social life mainly revolved around work during that period. Chester and I, while not the social butterflies, were great pals. There wasn't much room for socializing or sharing stories and laughter with others. [2]During my time at DVI with Mike, we often dreamed about our wild nights out post-release, envisioning partying, drinking, and charming the ladies. However, that fantasy never materialized. Mike had long been released from DVI, and I suppose Vicki tamed that adventurous spirit of his.

It was the end of the month, and that was bad. Eastland I, the cash cow, continued to paint ten cars daily. Half of those cars required fast bodywork. That business kept us afloat until the calendar rolled around to the day to pay the suppliers.

Jose gave me half of anything he got paid on after deducting

---

2. When I was eighteen, a judge sent me to DVI, Deuel Vocational Institution—a place I insist is a prison, far from anything resembling juvenile hall. In total, I spent about 27 months incarcerated, locked away as my past decisions haunted me, not all those months at DVI.

parts. To keep it simple, he paid for his parts. If he didn't have the money, I gave it to him out of pocket, and he paid me after the job was completed. I did not want the mechanic department to become another debt to a supplier. It was free and clear when Jose gave me fifty dollars for my share. He did not use Eastland invoices when he started, so I didn't have to deal with sales tax. I told my accountant if Jose's income became substantial, I would make it an official part of Eastland. It didn't take long for that to happen.

Gil came back to the main shop, and I sent Alexa to Eastland II. She was not ready to do complicated insurance estimates but was good at selling paint jobs. If a person needed an insurance estimate, she gave them a card with a note that the five-dollar estimate fee was waived. That gave the person an incentive to drive a mile to Eastland I. If all they wanted was a paint job, Alexa would do the selling there, write an estimate, and the customer could bring it to our main shop the following day.

"I talk to a lot of people," Alexa told Elena.

"Are you bored there?"

"Not bored if I'm busy," she said.

I heard from Elena again that we didn't need anyone at that shop.

MIKE'S STAMINA and strength were outstanding. If he had a free minute or two, he would do pushups between the restroom doors and the office stairs, just as he had done in the county jail and DVI. When Mike wanted to take off a day or two, he gave me a day's notice and took off with pay. He shined at Eastland. He worked Saturdays and got paid extra for it.

6

IS THIS WHAT MARRIED COUPLES DO

Elena and I took a Saturday off. We planned to sleep in, but we didn't. It was still dark when I put on my shorts and tennis shoes.

"I want to go with you," Elena said. "Wait for me."

I was surprised by her interest. This was the first time she wanted to jog since she had quit halfway up the hill. Every night, she would say she was going to jog with me the next morning, but when morning came, it never happened—until now.

"Do we need to do that damn mountain?"

"No mountain," I said. "Flatland."

"I won't poop out. I promise."

I sat at the foot of the bed and waited as she pulled a tee over her head and put on a pair of socks and tennis.

Elena turned to me, a playful spark in her eyes, a touch of curiosity in her voice. "Is this what married couples do?" she asked her tone a mix of amusement and genuine curiosity. "Jog together in the early morning light, share intimate moments, and fuck five or more times a day?"

"For the first few months of marriage. After that, forget it."

"What a terrible outlook on marriage G."

"Baby, what am I supposed to say? I been married three times!."

Elena was on her feet and ready to go. "G, if this is our honeymoon, I don't want it to end."

We kissed. It was a kiss where our teeth lightly grazed each other.

"I really love having you here with me," I said.

"I love it too."

"We better start the jog before we end up in bed again."

We laughed and headed out.

Elena & George

She did a decent job on the flat run. I could have gone longer, but there was no need to go crazy.

When we were back at the apartment, we had coffee, toast, and cream cheese. It was fun to fix breakfast together, the back-and-forth, using the toaster, making the coffee, and putting out silverware. It was very domestic and cozy. I put the silverware on the table. She poured the coffee. We had mismatched but familiar cups and saucers that had come from my mother's house.

We weren't breakfast people, but it felt right to eat together with time to burn that morning. I told her about when I first met Ava and Emma, when I had just moved in, and Emma had surprised me with a huge breakfast she'd cooked herself.

"It was a killer omelet, and I'm not even an egg eater. She was a short-order chef at Denny's for a long time."

"She quit to hook?"

"I don't know if she quit to hook," I said.

"Did you tell me you had a threesome with them?"

"You're thinking of Alicia and Clara."

"Who can keep track," she sighed and reached across to pinch my nose.

"Ouch," I said.

She gave me an oh come on look. It was hard for me not to think about her fucking Mike. I wondered where they did it. What position did they do it in? How long did he last? One of these days, I need to ask her all this.

ELENA and I had been living together long enough to develop a comfortable routine. Our days often began with a morning jog, a shared ritual that set the tone for the rest of the day. Typically, our Saturdays were no different—just a quick jog followed by a simple cup of coffee. But that particular Saturday broke the mold in the most delightful way.

Instead of our usual coffee, we decided to indulge in a hearty breakfast together. The aroma of freshly brewed coffee mingled with the scent of sizzling bacon and eggs, filling the kitchen with a warmth that mirrored our growing intimacy. After breakfast, we usually retreated to our separate showers—me to the master bedroom's en suite and Elena to the guest bathroom. But that Saturday, we chose to share the shower in the master bathroom.

The experience was both comical and intimate. We lingered under the warm spray, enjoying the closeness and the playful banter. Time seemed to slip away, and before we knew it, the hot water ran out. We found ourselves covered in soap suds, looking like a pair of yetis. The sudden burst of cold water was a shock to our systems, eliciting shrieks and laughter as we hurried to rinse off. Our naked bodies brushed against each other, adding a layer of sensuality to the hilarity of the moment.

After the chilly rinse, we took our time toweling each other dry, the soft fabric gliding over our skin, turning a mundane task into an act of tenderness. It was in these small, unexpected moments that I realized how deeply our lives had intertwined, creating a tapestry of shared experiences and unspoken understanding.

If this was our honeymoon, I wanted it to last and last.

"Where do you want to go?"

"Let's swim," she said.

"I'll take you anywhere. We can drive to the beach."

"G, I want to spend time with you here."

"I'm all for it, baby."

It was a pretty day, sunny and dry. It was still quite early, no one else by the pool, so we had it to ourselves. We dropped our towels and sunscreen in a couple of lounges, got in the water, and, after we started splashing around, saw Ava and Emma waving at us through their living room window.

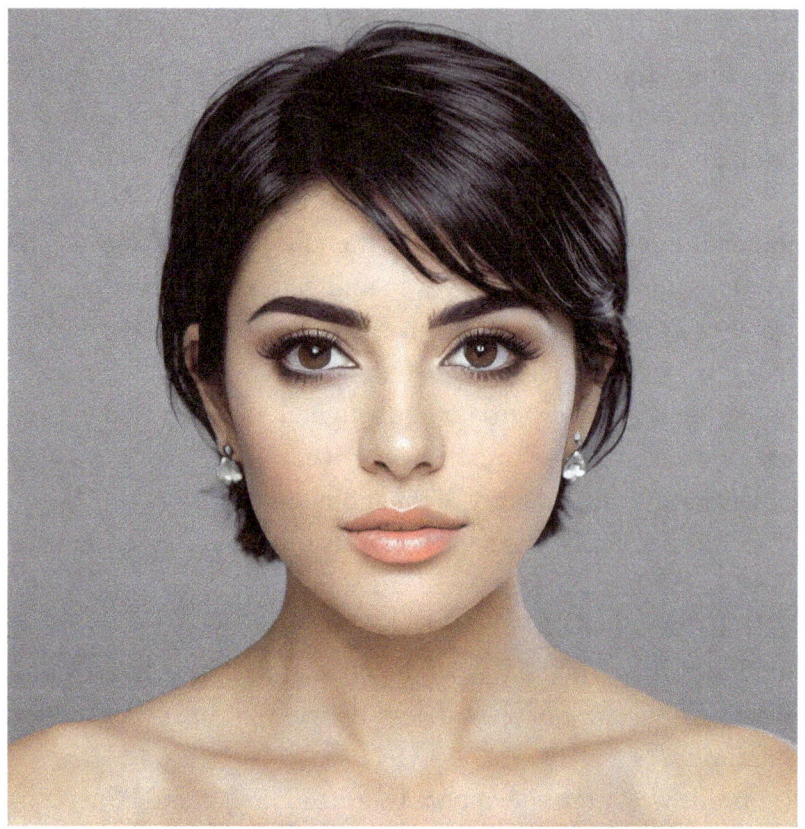

Ava

"I'm surprised they aren't asleep," I said to Elena as we waved back.

"Which one are you gawking at?" Elena asked, laughing and splashing me.

To think I didn't like red hair before. I was gawking at Emma.

Emma

I hadn't realized I was staring, but I was. "Elena, it's just me. Sorry."

"And you accuse me of flirting," she teased.

"No question, you're a flirt," I replied, still waving at Emma. "You never mentioned David, the guy from Hawaii."

"We were too busy enjoying Acapulco," she said, swimming to the far end of the pool and back. "I loved our trip—I had such a blast."

"We can do it again whenever you want," I offered.

"But you have so much business, and the cash flow is a mess."

"You sound like me," I laughed.

She hugged me tightly. "I want to sound like you." Then we kissed.

"Tell me about David."

"Right now, here in the pool?"

I took in her wet face, her hair clinging to her skin, no makeup. The sunlight hit her eyes, breasts, and shoulders, making them glimmer. Her bikini was giving me ideas, and I didn't really want to talk—I wanted to go inside and indulge in each other.

"You're beautiful."

She reached for my damp hair, which curled more when wet.

"You are beautiful," she countered, reading my thoughts. "Let's bail, hit your bed, and get wild."

Still smelling of chlorine and coconut oil, we ended up on the unmade bed, her on top, as if competing for the triple crown.

"Let's take it slow," she suggested, gazing down at me.

So we turned onto our sides, facing each other.

"You're in control," I said. "Steer however you like."

Being your own boss definitely has its perks, but the freedom to take off whenever you please isn't one of them—not if you want to keep the wheels turning smoothly. I'm referring to a small business.

I was lucky that everything at the shop had run like clockwork while we'd been away in Acapulco. I had to catch up with bank deposits for the week we were gone, but that was no surprise. All else was okay. The bills were paid, and no emergencies had come up. Mike had done very well.

THE SHEETS and blankets were in a heap on the floor. The fan was blowing on our naked bodies, and the room smelled like sex, coconut, and sun. We were cuddled together, then Elena rolled on her back and started moving her legs like she was walking.

"Where are you walking to?" I asked.

"My aunt's house."

"It's pretty close to the shop," I said.

She quit walking, sat up on the bed cross-legged, and ran her fingers through my hair. "Did I ever tell you why I came to the shop and asked you for a job?"

"I don't think so," I said, sitting up to face her.

"I used to walk to Safeway from the house. From way across the street, I saw this guy with curly hair. I noticed him there daily, with his curly hair, white T-shirt, and jeans. I asked the Safeway cashiers I know at the market about that guy. They talked about how young the boss was and how the corner was no longer an eyesore."

"I've only been in the market a couple of times," I said. "My first time in there, I met the manager and got his permission to park the loan cars in his parking lot."

"The cashiers know you."

"You haven't said why you came looking for a job."

"I was looking for a job, but that wasn't the main reason I went over there that day. I went there to meet you."

I leaned forward till our noses bumped and kissed her. "I'm glad you came over, that's for sure."

"I'm gladder," she said.

"I never asked why Ramirez's son pounced on me."

"We went on five dates. I met him at the liquor store next to the mortuary. I had met his father and saw the resemblance. I cut it off, and he kept calling me. He was still calling after I had gone to work for you. The morning he came to the shop, I had a call from him an hour before, and I hung up on him."

"He figured I'd stolen you from him."

"I didn't tell him that. He's good-looking but not half as good-looking as he thinks he is. He's a big mouth, a pothead, a hothead, and in training to be a drunk like his daddy."

"Ouch," I said.

"I hate him for ambushing you like he did."

"He didn't do anything to me that he didn't get paid back for that day."

Elena's eyes sparkled, and the hint of a grin curled the corners of her lips. She nodded.

"You kicked his ass."

"The ass-beating cost me, Ramirez."

"He did you a favor."

We ordered a pizza, calzone, spaghetti, and meatballs delivered from Dominos. I tossed the pizza box on the bed.

"Need to get a cover for the pretty sheets," Elena said.

"There's more where these came from."

"The locker thing?" Elena asked.

I grinned, nodding.

She went across the hall, came back with a big towel, and wafted it over the bed.

"Tablecloth, Your Highness, king of the locker thing," she put the to-go boxes on the terrycloth. We ate in bed with cokes from the refrigerator and china plates on top of a towel as if we were camping on the mattress.

"What did you give Hawaii guy in return for letting you live in luxury for six months?"

She downed the last of a Coke. "Hawaii guy got it all," she shrugged. "He had me for breakfast, lunch, and dinner. He got it all."

"No wonder he didn't want to let you go."

She grinned, "Are you jealous?"

"Not jealous," I said with a grin of my own. "I didn't know you then."

"Does that mean you'd be jealous if I did it again now that you know me?"

I didn't answer right away. I was thinking of how she admitted having sex with Mike right after she did it.

"I'd be jealous," I admitted.

WE GOT UP, teamed together, rolled up the dirty bedding, and put it in the laundry bag. I was in skivvies, and she was in red panties. When we made the bed, we laughed a lot as I showed her again the Navy method of folding the forty-five-degree angle at the corners of the mattress bottom and how I got the sheets as tight as I did. Getting a quarter to bounce off the top sheet on a big bed can be challenging, but it could be done.

The quarter bounced, sort of.

"So, while you were doing your locker thing," Elena said, "And your Navy thing, and all of your other things, I spent months studying to become a mortician."

I threw myself on the bed we had just made up, pulled the pillow up to make a backrest, laced my fingers, and folded my arms behind my head, a perfect listening position.

"Tell me you're kidding."

"Nope. My aunt never asked me any questions, but she did say I could live at home for free when I got back from Hawaii. However, if I wanted money like what she gave me for the trip, I had to work at the mortuary.

I had already spent some time working in the office after

school, so I knew the ropes. So, I asked her, 'Are you trying to tell me something?'

'Not trying, I am flat out telling you,' she replied firmly. 'Get in the family business. Your mother was an embalmer, a mortician, a funeral director. I followed in her footsteps, and your brother is almost there.'

'No way,' I told her, shaking my head. To be what she wanted me to be, I needed, at the very least, an associate degree, and I wasn't going back to school.

Then she explained what I already knew: as long as I worked in the business and logged hours under a monitor, I could choose my path without attending mortician school. The catch was that I had to pass a state exam to get licensed."

"You are filled with surprises," I said.

"I put in one year of college and didn't go back. I started doing makeup for the decedents. I felt like I was giving them some dignity back. My aunt was happy. She wanted me to follow in my mom's footsteps or her own steps or my brother, who is all in on it."

"Is there a lot of money in that business?" I asked.

"Yes, there is a lot of money in it."

"More than painting cars?"

"With a lot of overhead," she said. "If you only handle one funeral at a time, it's not so bad. If you can do four funerals simultaneously like we do, you need a lot of cars and employees."

I didn't ask how much a hearse cost, but I'm sure it was three or four times as much as my Impala.

"You are one tough lady," I said. "I'm not sure I could handle the dead, day in, day out."

"I am not afraid of the dead," she said. "I am more afraid of the living. The living go mad or intentionally set out to hurt or kill. A dead person can't do you any harm."

We sat back on the bed, the television flickering in the background, though we weren't really watching it. Our conversation flowed easily, punctuated by the occasional glance at the screen. Saturday morning cartoons were a cherished ritual, a burst of color and fun to kick off the weekend. Back then, there was no such thing as a mute button; instead, a simple dial controlled the volume. But no one ever turned the TV on with the sound off—it was all part of the experience.

Television in the sixties was a mixed bag. There were only three main stations: ABC, NBC, and CBS. Public broadcasting was still in its infancy and didn't quite count similarly. Each of the three networks had their own morning news and six o'clock news programs. In the evenings, they would each air a movie, and the rest of the time was filled with sports or series shows that ran for either thirty or sixty minutes. Everything was free but constantly interrupted by commercials.

If you were a fan of a particular series, you had to make sure you were in front of the TV at its scheduled time. There were no reruns or on-demand options—if you missed an episode, you missed it, and you'd have to wait a whole week to catch the next one. Dedicated viewers made it a point to be parked in front of the TV at the specified time.

On Sundays, the newspaper included a paperbound newsprint magazine with all of the week's shows. Every daily newspaper also had the day's TV schedule. For those who wanted more detailed information, there was the TV Guide magazine, available by subscription or at the grocery store. We weren't TV or sports fanatics, so we usually made do with the Sunday guide.

Most of the time, we didn't pay much attention to the TV unless it was a movie. There were no CDs or DVDs back then. If you wanted to watch a movie, you either caught it on TV or went out to the theater and made a night of it. It was a different era, one where television was a communal experience, and planning your viewing was part of the fun.

ELENA KISSED ME. It was not a tremendous kiss, but a kiss just the same. A smoking commercial followed, followed by a car commercial.

"Do you want me to buy you a car?"

"I don't need a car, not right now. I prefer riding with you."

I meant it. I had great credit. I'd buy her a car in a heartbeat. It was my turn to kiss her.

"Not even a hearse?" I asked, tickling her between the ribs. "Do you want a hearse?"

She laughed and shook her head no. "Did I ever tell you that I got a DUI?"

"Drunk driving? Say it ain't so."

"I was in junior college. When I got back from Hawaii, I was used to drinking with Mr. Hawaii guy when he was there, and when he was away, I drank all the time. In Hawaii, I didn't have to drive. I got home and thought I could do it here while I was driving my aunt's car. I got popped on Olympic Boulevard."

"What happened?"

"When I sobered up, they released me without having to

post bail. My aunt sent her lawyer to court with me. The judge chewed me out, but he didn't give me jail time or probation. He fined me three hundred dollars. He had a reputation for being mean. My lawyer kept telling me not to worry, but I was worried. I believed if I was sent to jail, I'd get raped by the women there."

"You did not think that," I said, laughing first.

"How does a woman rape another woman?" Elena said, shrugging.

"Out here or in prison?"

I got hit by a pillow.

We exchanged a lot of stories.

"When I left Hawaii, Mr. Hawaii gave me five thousand dollars in hundred-dollar bills. It was a surprise. I wasn't with him for money," she said.

"Did you give the money back?"

"Not a fucking chance."

I laughed so hard it made her laugh. Have you tried kissing when you are laughing hard? It's hilarious.

"Smart," I said.

"I don't spend much. I get pedicures and manicures."

"Who does that fabulous hair I love so much?"

"You looking at who does it."

"You got to be kidding."

"You just haven't caught me doing it."

"Amazing."

"Not amazing at all. All I need is a good pair of scissors and two mirrors."

We laughed and rolled around the big bed, tickling, laughing, kissing.

"Can I ask you something about the family business?"

"Anything."

"Did you do the nails of the dead?"

"Yes," she replied. "It's part of giving the person their dignity, to look as good as possible to the very last detail. People who view their loved ones notice things like that, and they will feel good about it."

"Why did you stop working at the mortuary?"

"For me, it was a long time. I was at the point where I was talking to myself because there was no one around who was alive that I could talk to. When I started talking to the decedents, I knew I'd had it. I quit."

"What did your aunt say?"

"She said I'd be back."

I thought about her doing makeup and nails on corpses.

"You know what I think about that mortuary make-up job? You are kind," I said.

"I just want to be good at whatever I'm doing. I put my heart in it."

"Yes, it's true." I nodded. "You've become a knowledgeable service manager who can do it all, even auto collision estimates for insurance claims."

"You do the same, and you do it better," she said.

I kissed her for the two hundredth time that day.

"You really dig learning mechanic work. I see you over with Jose a lot."

"I need to know what I'm talking about. I can't bid the work unless I know what I'm doing. Mauro was right. Jose is a good mechanic. He's young, and he's damn good. He's teaching me as we move along."

As I had learned watching Luis in the paint booth, I also did with Jose. I got into the nitty gritty. I knew the workings of a tune-up, carburetors, starters, and solenoids, how to test a battery, and how to check for burned fuses. I got a good look at a transmission as Jose was rebuilding it. I watched him hoist a rusted-out seized-up motor out of an old Ford and replace it with a practically new motor he bought at a junkyard. I was amazed at the work. He made it look easy, but I guess it is easy if you know where all the pieces go under the hood. Jose pointed out how some cars are inconveniently assembled, so sometimes, you have to take out or move some big thing to get at some small commonplace, other thing.

7

A THIRD LOCATION

I never told my banker about Chester being my backup. There was no reason for him to know. Holmberg's bank didn't make short-term unsecured loans. He told me that himself.

I wasn't going back to my parents to get three thousand I had paid back, so at least once a month, I hit Chester for money and gave him checks to hold. The hold time was getting longer. I felt that if I had another paint shop, the cash flow from that would help carry the lag in collections of Eastland's insurance collision repairs.

I kept looking for a building to house another paint shop. Next door to a Sears store, I found a large warehouse in Los Angeles on Soto Street. The building was roomy enough for a spray booth and oven, with plenty of work areas for bodywork.

Elena couldn't conceal her enthusiasm.

"I love it, but you don't have the cash," she said.

"I have credit to get the equipment. I can swing paying to lease the place and the rest, I can buy it on credit."

"Swing it means you cash a check then run to make a deposit by cashing another check." She laughed.

I didn't laugh. She was correct.

"Give it a chance," I said.

"Credit means you need to pay in thirty days," Elena said. "Then what?"

"Then, I'll float a bigger amount from Chester."

"I have five you can have," she said. "Could be lucky money for you."

"No way. I'm not borrowing money from people I know and love."

I could never forget the loan I got from Patty's mom. It was a thirty-five hundred dollar loan that I borrowed under false pretenses, and I ended up going to prison for it. Some would say that DVI (Deuel Vocational Institution) is not a prison; it's juvenile detention, but that's a lie. It's a prison—a prison with gun towers all around it.

THAT AFTERNOON, Elena got on the phone with three insurance companies that owed me $45,000[1]. That was a ton of money to be down at one time. My profit was tied up in jobs completed but unpaid.

In the morning, Elena collected a little over five thousand as a result of her calls.

Before I committed to leasing the Soto property, I called my spray booth person and the company that sold me the oven and asked them to survey the building and give me an installation proposal. The installation had to include all city permits.

When I made my daily bank deposit, I showed Holmberg

---

1. Adjusted for inflation, $45,000.00 in 1962 is equal to $385,461.00 in 2020.

four pictures of the property. He said he would cover the spray booth, oven, and any large equipment I needed to buy. I didn't need much else to make it a paint shop, only about two thousand for signage and painting the exterior of the building. It didn't have fabulous lighting, but it was good enough. I didn't have to buy anyone out, and the location was great.

"You need two salespeople like us," Elena said, "Who?"

"You just said it. You and me. Mike and Gil can handle it here."

She made a sad face.

"Oh, baby, I love it here."

"Okay, I'll send Mike and Gil there."

Elena clapped. She didn't go to her aunt's house often, but it was a seven-minute walk if she wanted to.

We started looking around to put a crew together at Eastland III. Elena and I timed our drive from the first shop to the new shop. It took fifteen minutes without traffic. Traffic coming in and out of the Sears parking lot could delay the drive by more than five minutes.

IN TWO MONTHS, we had a grand opening. Elena cut a deal with Pepe, a DJ at a very popular Spanish radio station, on a series of commercials. The hook he suggested was that a customer could drop off their car and have it painted while they shopped at Sears. It was true, but of course, the actual time depended on how many cars were in the queue.

The new shop painted five cars on the first day. We painted double that at the main shop. The next day, five cars again. Without the commercials, we could be dead.

"Maybe it's a five-cars-a-day shop," Elena said.

"Baby, it's too soon to say that."

On the third day, we painted four cars. The following day, we were back to five.

"You got to count on there being a little bodywork on almost every job," Mike said. "Average is fifty dollars per car."

"Good point. I'm not bitching." But I was bitching.

Eastland, our cash cow, continued to paint ten cars a day. Unfortunately, Elena turned out to be right that the new shop was a five-cars-a-day shop. It had expenses: rent, utilities, insurance, payroll taxes plus payroll for the crew: Gil, Mike, a painter, a painter's helper, and a bodyman.

Having the other shop took getting used to. When I expanded, I hadn't thought about getting their sales money every day and preparing a deposit. Elena helped me.

"I need to give you a raise or make you a partner," I said. She was seated across from me, helping with the deposits.

"What kind of partner?" Her eyes went wide. "Business or life?"

"If I wasn't already married, I'd ask you to marry me," I said.

"My aunt told me we should get married."

"She doesn't even know me," I said, "You know we've never met. If she knew I'd been married three times and about to get another divorce, she'd change her mind in a heartbeat. What made her say that?"

"I think she's impressed that I'm working with you and living with you, and she hears about you. It's a big neighborhood, and the buzz is constant. She hears things, like that people like you. Look at the people who come in because a friend referred them. My aunt knows everyone. She's the neighborhood undertaker."

"That sounds kind of creepy," I said.

"She's not very social outside the business, but for her family is everything. I know she loves me. She wants me to be happy. Since I've been with you, she sees me as being calm, cool, and collected. That's not how she usually sees me. She credits you for that."

"Wow," I said.

She walked around to where I was sitting. I stopped what I was doing and turned in my swivel chair. She sat on my lap and put her arms around me. We kissed.

"You're so bad, G," she said.

"You right, I'm bad."

"I love bad," she said. "Marriage would fuck up the wonderful thing we have going. We're not getting married."

"Elena, three times I was convinced that marriage was the right thing to do. The first time, I was just a kid of seventeen with no money, and I belonged to the US Navy. I married a gorgeous woman four years older than me without giving it a second thought. She didn't really want to get married, but I kept on and on until she agreed. I am such a dummy." I sighed. "I agree, marriage would fuck up the wonderful thing we have going."

"Your second marriage went on for less than a month, and you got divorced?" Elena chuckled. "I'm not laughing at you. I'm laughing at how young you were, and you got married again after the first one failed."

"And then I went and got married again. My present wife is way too good for me. She just wants to be a wife, and that's not good enough for me."

"I know; you've told me before how good she is, and your daughter is adorable. You should get updated pictures of her."

"I don't even see her that often, but you're right. I will."

"G, don't stress. Marriage is not for me either. At least not now or in the near future. I love being with you." Her kiss was slow and passionate.

I thought about my first wife, Selena, my first wife. Alicia, my second wife. Sophia, my third wife. I pictured their faces. I had the scent of Selena causing a stir as it always did.

"Where are you?" Elena asked.

"Marriage talk makes my brain wander. Sorry."

"You do that a lot."

"Sorry. I was thinking of my marriage-checkered past."

"I love you, Elena."

Elena opened her eyes wide, seemingly surprised. "G, I'm sure that's the first time you told me that."

"It's not the first time," I said. "Not the first time."

We hugged.

"Let's finish up and go home," she said with her all-time smile.

IT WAS OPENING TIME. The gates were open; the shop coffee was percolating, and everyone was on task.

"I might pull Gil back," I said. "Mike can handle it alone."

"I wouldn't," Elena said. "It may get busier." She winked, kidding. We both knew the new shop was a five-cars-a-day shop, period. The only reason I opened that shop was to make more money. I knew already it was not going to happen. I was such a dummy.

Elena took the next customer. She walked up to the thirty-plus lady with her arm extended.

"Good morning, welcome. My name is Elena. How can I help you?"

I thought how well Elena fit in here. She could be doing anything somewhere other than an auto paint shop in East Los Angeles. Why would she be sticking it out with me? Certainly not for the little bit of money I paid her.

A customer got out of a car and walked up to me. She looked to me like a housewife.

"Are you George?" she asked.

"I am," I said, going for the handshake. She was dressed casually, looked tired, and had a ring on her finger.

"Jimmy Duran referred me. He said you did a fine job on his car."

"I remember Jimmy," I lied with a smile. "Would you like a cup of coffee?"

AS USUAL, two hours later, we had processed the day's ten cars. Today's lineup consisted entirely of paint jobs, with six requiring minor bodywork. Once we met our daily quota, we either scheduled additional work for another day or the customers left their cars with us. People didn't seem to mind. Our mechanic work was at full capacity. Jose could have used more car stalls, but I couldn't allocate any more space. He almost always had cars waiting outside to be worked on.

"If I had any sense, I'd quit this insurance work," I confided to Elena over lunch. Certainly not the first time. "I'd focus solely on painting. Cash in hand, no more waiting for payments."

Elena's eyes lit up. "Can we start today?"

I frowned, meeting her gaze. "I said if I had any sense." We both laughed. "The real money is in the insurance work, not the thirty-five dollar paint jobs. It takes time, but when those checks finally come in, it's worth it."

"G, don't overlook the money you pay Chester to hold the checks to tide you over each month. It's not cheap. It digs into that money that finally comes in from the insurance carriers."

"Believe me, I don't overlook that expense. It's hefty. We still come out with a profit, I'm sure of it."

"Whenever you want to do the math and check it out. I'm here to help," Elena said with a wink. She kept right up with me. No question. She was smart.

You can't judge a book by its cover, and you can't gauge a shop's success by its curb appeal. I had fallen in love with the shop next to Sears, but it had let me down. Maybe the first shop was thriving because I was there from opening to closing. Perhaps the magic formula was Elena and me. If we were at the other shop, would it still be a five-cars-a-day shop? It felt unfair to my friend Mike to even consider that. Mike was a hard worker, and I was confident he was doing his best. But no matter how hard you work, success depends on the business coming through the door.

I kept hitting Chester for money to make it even out. At least I never failed to come through for both of us. The amount was no longer under ten thousand. One month I hit him for twelve thousand dollars and gave him two six-thousand-dollar checks to hold and a hundred for himself.

It's amazing the trust that builds when you don't fail. Chester never hesitated, and his lack of hesitation had nothing to do with the little extra I was giving him. My accountant wrote a flood of checks to pay the bills of not one shop but three. Chester gave me a ton of money that I'd take to the bank the next day and deposit. Shop two was a minor expense, but still, there was rent, utilities, insurance, and one employee.

Chester stopped by one day at about noon to buy tacos next door. He was a happy-go-lucky kind of guy that gave off a jolly vibe. He was always smiling. Elena and I were in a huddle near the front entrance. We had no new customers, but there were four in the waiting room.

"I noticed that when I tell you to deposit a check, it sometimes takes four days or more to get to my bank. I call every morning for a balance, and I have this big balance, much larger than my book balance," I said.

"That's float," Chester said. "You're right. Even if we bank at the same bank but at a different branch, it takes two days to get to your branch. We bank at Commerce Bank, and you're at Bank of America. When I deposit your check today, it won't be there for four days. If I deposit it on a Friday, add another two days."

"I don't know why I like that so much," I said. "I need to digest it."

Elena laughed and made the sign of the cross. "Chess, I think you just started something."

The quickie was supposed to be just that, a quickie. It had been as fast as the name implies, and we were in the office on the sofa, recuperating. I was staring at the ceiling, thinking about floating checks.

"Are you thinking about the float or about my fine ass?" Elena asked.

Took a second, maybe two, for me to say, "Your fine ass, baby. I love, love, love it."

8

SUSIE

I bit the bullet and did not bring Gil, hoping optimistically that he and Mike could increase the volume of jobs or the average sale to more than fifty dollars.

Elena and I needed help.

I interviewed a twenty-four-year-old girl named Susie. Instead of going up to the office, Elena, Susie, and I sat in the area downstairs where customers waited. It was early in the day, but a car was being painted already, and one was being masked. Our voices rose and fell in competition with the noisy shop.

"What makes you think you can do this job?" I asked.

"I worked for Eric Hughes for the past two years. I started masking cars, went to estimating, writing insurance estimates, and worked up to assistant manager at the Torrance paint shop."

"Why aren't you there anymore?"

"I make seventy-five dollars a week. I was told I had gone as far as I could. I'm looking for more."

"Tell you what, Susie. I'll start you here with Elena and me. If you can cut it in five weeks, I'll pay you a hundred a week, and we can move on from there."

"You will love me," Susie said. She gave Elena and me both the eye. Not the evil eye, the flirty eye. I noticed cats eye eyeliner and fake eyelashes. I don't usually notice that kind of thing, but it was pretty obvious. I raised my eyebrows and looked at Elena.

"Susie, are you a flirt?" Elena asked, trying to be sober and employer-like.

"Not if you don't want me to be. Should I call you Jefa[1]?"

Elena tried and failed to keep a straight face. "A girl like you is going to be constantly hit on," Elena said. "That's a compliment. It can cause distraction in your work. We can't have that."

---

1. Jefa a feminine boss

"I won't let it cause distraction." She switched to Spanish. "Have you looked in a full-length mirror lately? You're stunning. Me, I'm a pencil next to you."

Elena looked down at her cleavage, then over Susie's head to me. Charisma recognizes charisma. "Susie has some con in her," Elena said. "That makes for great sales."

"You're hired, Susie. Let's see how good you really are." I said my hand out for a shake.

THAT NIGHT, we picked up cokes and pastrami from The Hat and took them home to the kitchen table.

I munched away.

Elena said, "If I liked girls, I would fuck Susie. I find her adorable." She grinned at me mischievously.

Of course, as soon as she said it, I pictured it.

"You know what I'm seeing in my head right now, right?" I said, going for a couple of fries. "I love you to talk dirty like that. Do it more often?"

"I'll work on that."

I watched her take a good chunk of the pastrami in her mouth. A pickle slice would have dropped on the table, but she caught it and put it in her mouth.

"You're staring," she said playfully, doing pickle gymnastics in her mouth. I saw a sparkle in her eyes as she met mine.

"I know," I said.

SUSIE WAS EXPERIENCED in our field. Her training was only about how we did things at Eastland. She didn't need training to sell paintwork or bodywork or write insurance estimates for wrecked cars.

9

JUDGE BLACK

The mayor of a small local town came in. He was a modest guy, and no one would have known he was a mayor except that one of the helpers recognized him. The mayor referred us to a city council member, who referred us to his secretary. Word of mouth is a real thing.

I was writing an insurance estimate when Elena came over to me and pointed out a marshal's car driving in, followed by a T-bird.

"That's Judge Black," she said. "He was the judge on my DUI. Meanest son-of-a-bitch in East LA. Been there twenty years or more. Sends everyone to jail. I don't know why he spared me."

"He brought the heat with him," I said, chuckling.

As I continued writing an insurance estimate, Susie talked to the two men and then came over to me.

"Judge Black wants to meet you. A court clerk referred him to Eastland."

Pages of Passion Book 3: Rising Waves

Judge Harold Black was about sixty. He looked like a Harry Truman impersonator and had the same gruff, no-nonsense personality. He talked around an ever-present cigar. His were a more expensive brand than the ones Ramirez used to chew on.

After we closed, I went next door to pick up a couple of steaks for dinner. I picked out a couple in the case upfront. Chris was sweeping up for the night.

"Hang on," Jesse said. "Let me get you a couple real steaks." He disappeared through the doors and came out with a couple of porterhouses that were thicker, bigger, and more marbled than the ones I'd chosen. As he wrapped them in butcher paper, I told Jesse and Chris that Judge Black had dropped off his car. I got an earful from the brothers. According to them, he was a tough judge who came down hard on people perpetrating crimes upon innocent victims. Drunk drivers. Child neglecters. People like that. He meted out justice with stern self-righteousness. Off the bench, he had a reputation for being an eccentric.

"Do you know him personally?" I asked.

"Never met him. Thank God never been in his courtroom either. Everyone knows him."

Two days later, the judge returned for his car. It was in the early evening, and a young woman in a glossy red convertible had dropped him off. I'm pretty sure we'd done that paint job. The crew was finishing up for the day, which means they were organizing the first jobs for tomorrow, but all the other customers had gone.

He walked around his car, examining it closely.

"Doesn't look like the same car. Excellent work!" He spoke decisively and enunciated like every word was important. Or maybe that was just me knowing he was a judge.

"Thank you, judge."

"Now, if you'll give me my invoice, I'll settle up."

I waved my hand as he started to pull out his checkbook. I looked at my watch as if I was in a hurry.

"I'll bill you," I said.

I never billed him.

Eventually, he called me.

"Hatcher, you haven't sent me a bill for my paint job. Now I need tires. Do you sell them?"

"I sure do, Judge," I lied.

The next day, one marshal dropped off the judge's car, and another marshal followed him and drove him back to court. I called Goodyear, and Jose installed the tires.

Judge Black came personally to pick up his car.

"I'll bill you, Judge. Don't worry about it."

He gave me a knowing grin. "Thank you, Georgie."

"My pleasure."

The next time he called, he gave me a referral.

"Sending you a friend of mine, Teran. He's a superior court judge downtown. Be sure you send him a bill, understand?"

"Yes, Judge. Thank you."

"By the way, Hatcher, I want to invite you to accompany me to the Rotary Club. Get away from your shop for a couple of hours next Friday. If you like it, I'll sponsor you."

THAT NIGHT, we were sitting at the kitchen table. I put the ice cream out. Elena doled out the bowls. I scooped. She drizzled on chocolate syrup. I sprayed whipped cream.

I told Elena, "I'm not going to the Rotary Club with the judge. I don't even know him, and with my record, I can't do it."

I sat down. Elena held up a chocolate sandwich cookie and a home-made chunky chocolate chip.

I pointed at the chocolate chip. She crunched half over my sundae and half over hers.

"G, your record was a juvenile record; besides, no one is going to run a make on you."

I handed her a spoon and a napkin from the middle of the table, and we dug in.

"Juvenile or not," I said.

She took a bite, savoring for a full minute before she replied.

"Okay, I can call him and tell him that you don't have anyone to take over on that day. He'll understand."

"I'm going to take good care of you for doing that."

"What about the ice cream?"

"After," I said, aiming the whipped cream nozzle at her.

She laughed and put the dishes, spoons, and all in the freezer.

"After is fine."

After Elena called the judge, she came up to the office where I was preparing a deposit.

"I called the judge."

I put down the pen. "And?"

Elena brought a cup of coffee over, and put it on my desk and poured herself one. We had paper cups downstairs, but it's better in the mugs in my office.

"The clerk answered the phone. I told her I was calling on your behalf, and the next minute I was talking to the judge. I'm sure he took the call while he was on the bench doing his judging thing. I could hear something going on. People testifying and stuff like that."

I laughed.

"He said it's okay, but he wants to take you to lunch. He will call you."

I really didn't set out to befriend the judges and mayors and other politicians who were falling into Eastland like a line of dominoes. But once they fell in my lap, I looked after them in a grand way.

Finally, the day came when I couldn't excuse my way out of having lunch with Judge Black. I went home at eleven to change clothes into a suit and tie. The only reason I had a suit was because [1]Alicia said I should have one. I'd had a tailor hem it when I clipped it during the locker thing. In that suit, I drove to the East Los Angeles courthouse and found his courtroom. It was five minutes past noon, and court was in session. The judge saw me walk in. The room was full of an assortment of people.

---

1. Alicia was my second wife. My girlfriend for more than a year and my wife for about 24 days.

"Excuse me, counselors," he said into the microphone on the bench where he was presiding from. "Let's break for lunch. See you back at one forty-five."

He came out from behind his throne.

"Hi Georgie," he said. "Follow me to chambers, and we'll be off in a few minutes."

The marshal who had been to my shop before came up to greet me. He shook my hand and walked me to the back of the courtroom. I was beckoned to his chambers, where the judge had a mahogany coat tree, where he switched from his black robes to a suit coat. I got a quick glimpse of a big desk, sofa, pull-up chairs, flags, and a bookcase with law books. Like the courtroom, the walls were paneled in oak, and the carpet was nice. It felt awkward and dream-like and not quite real. A judge had sentenced me to the California Youth Authority. A marshal just escorted me to a judge's chambers. I watched him remove his robe and put on a suit jacket. For me. It felt surreal.

I DROVE the judge in my Impala.

"Your parents must be very proud of you," he said as we drove to Steven's Steakhouse, a seven-minute drive. "I hardly know you, and I'm proud of you."

"Thank you, judge. That's kind of you to say."

He laughed hoarsely.

He pulled a cigar from his inside jacket pocket and stuck it in his mouth.

"I'm not lighting it until after we have our lunch."

I chuckled. "The smoke doesn't bother me, judge."

"I understand you opened another shop on Soto over by Sears."

"Yes, sir, I did."

"George, it's okay to call me judge, but you don't need to sir me. We're friends."

"Yes, sir, got it," I said.

He laughed at me. He was putting me at ease. I mean, this guy was a judge with the power to send people to jail, just like that, and he was riding in my car, and we were going to have lunch together.

I felt crazy formal, but at least Steven's Steakhouse didn't have sterling flatware and charger plates. I could handle eating with Judge Black, thanks to lessons from my father.

"I live in Montebello, a short distance from the courthouse. It's a good city to live in, older but nice," he said.

"I live in Monterey Park."

"That's the Beverly Hills of East Los Angeles," he said, laughing.

He told me about his life growing up as a Jewish kid in a predominately Latin neighborhood. "I did okay. When I ran for office, God Bless the Latino community. They voted me in office, and I've been here a long time."

He asked about my history.

I told him about my apprenticeship at WESPAC, about my grumpy genius mentor Matt.

"When I gave him my two-week notice that I was going into business for myself, he took it personally. He says to me, 'Get off my roof this minute!'"

Judge Black laughed first, then got serious. "Have you invited him over to see what you've done?"

"I haven't."

"Call him," the judge said. "He may surprise you."

I nodded.

We ordered dessert. He had a banana split. I had two scoops of pistachio ice cream.

When the bill came, it was a battle that I won and the beginning of a friendship that lasted for many years. I was only a youngster, a nobody with a high school diploma that I obtained at DVI and a certificate of achievement in Refrigeration & Air-Conditioning that I received at DVI as well. He opened doors for me here and in Mexico. He introduced me to a whole new level of people, both in my shop and on a social level. That was incredible.

I WORE the suit back to the shop. Everything was as busy as it should be, but I didn't feel dressed right for the job. I stood in the area where I usually greet customers. It can get hectic sometimes, but it was pretty slow at that moment. Elena came over and played with my tie, something she could rarely do because I dressed up as infrequently as I could. "You look adorable."

"Susie, take over for a little while."

Elena and I went up to the office. Elena closed the louvers before she sat on the sofa, pulled me to her, and opened my zipper. She pulled it out and then worked me over. After a while, she pulled off my tie and my tucked-in shirt. What a way to get out of a suit.

I was all set to reciprocate, but Elena wanted a raincheck for that night. She handed me my t-shirt, jeans, socks, and tennis shoes, hung up my suit, and put a zippered cover on it for the ride.

When we were back on the floor, it was as Susie finished delivering a car.

"I see the Jefe changed clothes," Susie said.

It wasn't a secret. Elena had carried the suit out to put in the car, so we could drop it off at the laundry.

"Nosey you," Elena told her. "He got an oil change, too."

Susie grinned. She and Elena were getting tight.

10

FIRST TIME FOR EVERYTHING

Elena

One night, we closed a little later than scheduled. The team said their goodnights. Elena got behind the wheel to drive us. We were under a flood of parking lights. Inside, someone, probably Jessie, cut off the Market light. Everything was closing.

"I never asked if you have a car," I asked Susie

"It's fifteen minutes on the streetcar," she said.

"Want a ride?" Elena asked.

"I'm good. Have a good night."

She started walking toward Rowan Street to jaywalk across to the streetcar station.

"Susie, we're going to dinner," Elena yelled out the window. "Come with us."

I looked at Elena. I didn't have to ask the question aloud.

"She was like hanging around," Elena said in a low voice. "Like she was waiting for something."

Elena must have been right. Susie was already heading back to us.

"I'd love to go with you guys." She flashed her pearly whites.

I pulled my seat forward. Susie got in the back.

It was Friday night. Most young couples like Elena and me would be getting ready to go out partying at a club or something. Elena and I were like stay-at-home monks. Sure, we liked fun, laughs, and drinks, but we did all that at my apartment.

"Steven's Steakhouse where I had lunch with Judge Black has good food. Want to go there for a change?'

"Cool," Elena said. "It's Friday, so they have music and dancing."

"It's a cool spot," Susie said. "I been there."

"Me too," Elena said.

"I'm a terrible dancer," I warned with a chuckle.

WE WERE IN THE RESTAURANT. The live band was playing Mexican music, then American pop music. It was all loud but acceptable. A few older couples were dancing.

Susie suggested we try the beer Bohemia from Mexico. She

looked at the dancers and said, "If you're hungry and want good food, you come here. You don't come here to dance and party."

"She means it's not a place for young folks like us."

"I've been here one time, and it was for lunch with Judge Black," I reminded them.

"No complaints here," Susie said.

"Beats the Hat by a mile," Elena said through a mouthful of enchilada.

I had steak, rice, and refried beans. No tortillas for me.

Susie ordered two chile rellenos with rice and beans and flour tortillas.

"How'd you stay slim eating tortillas?" Elena asked Susie.

"How do you stay slim eating enchiladas?" Susie asked Elena.

"I fuck every day," Elena said. "Most mornings, I jog with G."

"Lucky you," Susie said, looking from Elena to me.

I said nothing to that.

We had one beer each. I wasn't much on beer anymore, but Bohemia seemed appropriate with the food. It was a strong dark beer. Even one will give you a buzz.

"This beer is potent, so you settle for one only," I said.

The girls laughed. We clicked bottles.

When the check came, Susie wanted to pay her share.

"Lighten up, girl," Elena said. "We invited you."

Elena was feeling the beer. I opened the door, and Susie got in the back seat. I would have opened the passenger door for Elena, but she got in too fast and laughed at me.

"Want a ride to your house, or you want to come over?" Elena asked Susie, her eyes twinkling with mischief.

"I got nothing going on at home," Susie replied, her voice carrying a hint of anticipation.

"G, I think she wants to join us," Elena said, nudging me with her elbow.

"Totally dig it," Susie chimed in, her smile broadening.

I slid behind the wheel and started the car, the engine purring to life. Elena fiddled with the radio dial until the smooth, melancholic strains of Bobby Vinton's "Blue Velvet" filled the car.

"Can you put the volume up a little?" Susie asked, leaning forward, her fingers tapping rhythmically on her knee.

Elena obliged, turning the knob until the music enveloped us. But I couldn't hear it. My mind was a whirlwind of thoughts—Susie and me at my apartment, Elena's enigmatic smile. What was she thinking? What was she planning? Memories of Alicia and Clara and our wild nights together flashed through my mind like a fever dream.

When we finally got home, Elena sauntered to the kitchen and returned with an open quart of Canadian Club. She raised the bottle, and Susie and I mirrored her gesture. CC and water for all of us, the ice clinking melodiously in our glasses. Not too heavy on the CC, just enough to warm our insides.

I carefully placed a stack of 45s on the turntable, the vinyl records gleaming under the dim light. The needle dropped, and the room was soon awash with the nostalgic tunes of the early sixties. I owned so many 45-rpm records back then that it was almost sinful.

Elena, sipping her CC and water, turned to Susie. "Hey Susie, what's happening in your personal life?"

"Not much to tell," Susie said, her voice tinged with a hint of melancholy. "Never been married. I inherited a small house when my mom died. I had three live-in relationships that all turned out badly. Since they were in my house, not the other way around, I got to show them the door. That's it. A short story."

"Great story," I said, already on my second drink. I was nestled between Elena and Susie on the sofa, the music weaving a tapestry of sound around us. They were mostly talking around me, their voices a comforting murmur.

"Where do you live?" Elena asked, leaning forward to catch Susie's eye. Her leg was crossed, and she held her glass delicately, resting it slightly on her knee.

"On Breed Street, over by Hollenbeck School," Susie replied.

"Hey, I went to that school," I said, a note of surprise in my voice.

"Me too," Susie said, her eyes lighting up.

That surprised me. I don't get surprised very easily. I instantly felt a connection to Susie, as if Hollenbeck had bestowed upon us a distant cousin status. Elena leaned across me to look at Susie, her eyes sparkling with curiosity. We weren't drunk but were feeling good, the warmth of the alcohol spreading through us.

"George has a bedroom no one uses," Elena said, her voice playful. "Want to stay for the night?"

Susie took a sip from her glass of CC, leaned forward, and looked over at Elena. "Where are you sleeping?"

"You got one guess," Elena said, laughing, her eyes dancing with amusement.

I was there in the middle of the conversation, appreciating it as it developed and not saying a word. I leaned against the back of the couch, my gaze shifting from left to right to whoever was speaking.

"Girl, I'm clean. Why you putting me in a bedroom alone?" Susie said, her voice teasing.

We all laughed, the sound mingling with the music, creating a symphony of camaraderie and shared moments.

It was the weekend when Mike took off for Las Vegas. He called me on Sunday night to brag about how he came back a winner.

"I kicked ass, "Mike said. "I made eight hundred dollars, and that was after I paid hotel and gas."

"What do you play?"

"Blackjack," he said.

I had played Blackjack at DVI. We played with stick matches for money. We were allowed matches because cigarettes were permitted as long as you bought them from the canteen.

"Who'd you go with?"

"Vicki. Who else?"

I had never been to Las Vegas.

"We're going next weekend," Mike said.

"You and Vicki?"

"No, you and me. I'll teach you Twenty-One. You'll love it. I know you'll be lucky!"

"I know how to play, but, yeah, give me all you got to teach."

We made our plans.

"Are you taking Elena?" he asked.

"Are you taking Vicki?"

"She's working two shifts."

Friday morning, I told Elena I was going to Vegas and wanted her to pal along.

"Come with us. It should be lots of fun."

"You go. I've been there. It will do you good to let your hair down."

"My hair is not long enough to let it down."

She whacked my arm, then ran her fingers through my hair, trying to mess it up.

"You gonna fly?"

"Damn, we're driving. You'll need a car."

"No sweat," she said. "I'll stay at my aunt's and walk to work. Stop worrying,"

11

LAS VEGAS

"**D**ouble down," Mike whispered as he looked at my cards. I followed his instructions. The dealer dealt me a card down. I got twenty-one.

Playing at DVI with match sticks for money, there were no rules.

I wish I hadn't done so well. Beginner's luck is the curse of the innocent. I came back with two thousand five hundred more than I had gone up with. I won more than that because I paid hotel, gas, and food from my winnings. I didn't get to see any of Las Vegas. We drove straight to the Flamingo and, two nights later, drove straight to Los Angeles.

Mike lost two hundred dollars, but he was still ahead. I risked more money than Mike, which was the only reason I won as much as I did.

I was full of the win. When I got home late Sunday night, I told Elena, "I won enough to buy you a new car."

"G, I don't need a car. Bank the money and tell Chester to clear a check."

I had planned to reduce the debt with Chester, but I would have given that up and bought a car for Elena had she told me she wanted one.

"I missed you," Elena said. "Did you miss me?"

"I couldn't sleep knowing Mike was in the other bed, and you weren't next to me on mine."

We kissed. We were in bed, and it was pretty late. Elena

reached over me and turned off the light on my side of the bed. We lay there in the dark, listening to the central air kick on and off.

"Did you pick up anyone in Vegas?"

"No way," I said. "And you, did you get some?"

"Not a chance. No one fucks me like you. What was the name of that girl you give all the credit to?"

"Christine," I said. "She was a Playboy cover girl."

"G, I heard the story."

"Well, I haven't heard the story of when you went to Vegas," I said.

"I was in junior college. I flew up with girlfriends."

"I think it's faster to drive when you figure the time to the airport and all that."

"We stayed at the Flamingo, like you did, got there on a Friday night, and made it back home by Sunday. While we were there, we were big-time tourists and took a taxi downtown. The lights there are incredible. The boulevard where the Flamingo is located is nothing like downtown."

"When I go up with you, we'll hit downtown," I said.

"I got lucky with craps," Elena said. "There was this big

Texan playing and losing. I kept watching him after my three friends moved on. He notices me and introduces himself. 'I'm Dan,' he says in this deep bass." She mimicked his deep voice. "He downs a drink and offers me the dice. I blow on the dice, then throw them, pretending like I've done it before. I blow, throw, and win. Each throw is a win for him and for half the table. I play it up, make a big deal of blowing on the dice, and damn, I go nine straight throws."

"That sounds like nine blackjacks."

"It looked like the Texas guy walked away with a bundle. But maybe he won some back or broke even. I don't know. What I do know is he gave me five hundred in hundred-dollar chips. I was elated,"

"That's two Texans. Hawaii and Vegas."

"I didn't fuck the Vegas Texan. But I did like craps. Do you?"

"I don't know about craps, but I feel good about blackjack. I thought I knew how to play, but nothing compared to Mike. Mike is a pro. He got me up and running."

"My aunt says that you can't beat the house."

"I heard that too, and I believe it. You have to win and walk."

"I guess. I don't know," Elena said. I felt her moving next to me and heard the soft swish of fabric. The gown she had been wearing in bed was now gone, and she was nude, skin-to-skin with me. "All I know is that when he gave me that five hundred dollars, I almost peed." Her mouth got close to my ear, and she whispered, "I had no panties on."

"Nasty girl," I said, pulling her gently to me. "In Vegas with no panties in the casino, at the foot of a crap table, probably bending over."

"I don't know about bending over. Next time I'm there, you have to remind me to bend over. Hey, say that again. I got chills thinking about it."

"Nasty girl. Bending over in Vegas," I said, "And what you did to Susie."

The memory got me hard.

"I gave you the same thing," Elena whispered. "You did her first. You had the hots for her."

"I had the hots for the both of you," I said. My lips were a quarter inch from hers. I loved her breath.

"I bet you want to do it again, don't you?"

"Only if you want," I said.

"I don't want. I feel funny," she said. "I'd never done that before."

"The day after we did it, we both said it was dynamite."

In the dark, I felt her nod against my chest.

"Is it uncomfortable working with her now?"

"Come on, I'm not a little girl."

"If it's uncomfortable, it's our secret," I said.

"It's uncomfortable, all right," she said, squirming and grabbing my hand. "If you don't believe it, touch me and see."

I pulled her body tighter against me. We kissed.

"Don't you dare call me Susie, either." She giggled.

"Don't you dare call me Mike."

She punched my chest. "That was a low blow," she said.

I grabbed between her legs. "How low?"

She sighed and moaned. "I love your fingers. You're driving me crazy."

EARLY SATURDAY MORNING, Elena drove me to the airport. The sky was a soft gradient of pink and orange, the sun just beginning to peek over the horizon, casting a warm glow on the sleepy city. The air was crisp, carrying the faint scent of dew.

"You should go with me," I said, knowing she had to work. "I can have Gil come over from Soto and help."

"You should have let Mike go with you," Elena replied, her voice tinged with concern as she navigated the labyrinthine streets around LAX, the car's engine humming.

"He's not coming this time. I can't afford to stake him. It's bad enough I'm getting Vegas fever."

"Go blow this hard-on you have for Vegas, once and for all."

"It's not that bad."

"Wait till you lose," she said, her tone a mix of teasing and warning.

"Elena, don't say that." I was driving but made the sign of the cross over my chest, the gesture feeling both comforting and futile.

She laughed, a light, melodic sound that momentarily lifted the tension. "Getting superstitious? Look, it would put us in a better position if we hired another floor person to work with Susie to give us a break," Elena said, her fingers drumming a soft rhythm on the steering wheel as we hit a patch of traffic.

"I'm bringing Gil back. When Mike wants to take off, we can send someone to cover."

"Deal," Elena said, her eyes flicking to mine with a hint of relief. "Listen, G, I watched players when I was in Vegas. Losers are not happy campers. One of the friends who went with me is from Vegas. She told me that there's a whole loser population, a whole Vegas culture supporting an army of pawnshops. Downtown, I lost count of the pawnshops. Bunch of broke and desperate losers, and the pond scum that makes an industry out of their desperation."

"I'm not a loser," I said, my voice firm but my stomach churning with unease.

"I didn't say you are. I just don't want you to have to take that hit. How much are you taking?"

"Two thousand."

When she kissed me goodbye through the window, her lips were warm and soft, but she caught my lip with her teeth, sending a jolt of surprise and pleasure through me. We both ended up laughing, the sound mingling with the distant roar of jet engines. I wished she was going with me.

"Elena, I want to say I love you, but I'm a loser at love."

Elena kissed me again, her lips lingering on mine, and I got out of the car with a hard ridge pressing against my zipper. As I walked away, I heard her say, "You love me," her voice a soft echo in the cool morning air.

My room had a king-sized bed overlooking the so-called strip, but there wasn't much to see.

Outside the hotel, there was a green awning surrounded by a chaos of glittering lights. Inside, the Flamingo was designed to dazzle. I was so focused on playing that the quality of light and flash, dazzle, and shiny bits were just a hypnotic background behind the games' unlimited potential.

As I was playing, I received free tickets to a show that I gave away later. I got a free pass to the buffet for two. If I had recorded the real-time gaming from two thousand down to five hundred, you would see some real nail-biting scenes. It was hopeless at five hundred. I could have, maybe should have stopped, should have walked away.

I started winning.

I came home Sunday with nine thousand. I took a taxi to my apartment. Elena was there, asleep on the couch. It was nice coming home to somebody there.

"I would have picked you up," she said, wiping the sleep from her eyes. She sat up in her little white shorts and crop top, stretching like a three-foot cat coming out of a one-foot box, and then lay down again with her head in my lap.

"This was easier," I said. "Ask me how much I won?"

"How much?" Big yawn.

Her eyes were closed. I pulled out a wad of hundreds and stuck it in her hands.

"What the hell?" she said, holding the cash and not opening her eyes.

"Nine big ones," I said.

SHE POURED us CC water in the living room and turned on the stereo to celebration music. I was jazzed.

"That's two wins in a row," Elena said. "Is it out of your system?"

I sighed. I kissed her. Elena's only enthusiasm was for my extreme hardness as I plunged inside. For me, it seemed there was just no aphrodisiac-like winning.

I deposited the money along with the weekend receipts from the two shops. I felt like I had a revelation that I could cure my cash flow problem in no time.

I called Chester.

"Hey friend, deposit all the checks. All good."

"Will do," he said.

I ONLY SAW Mike when I went over to the Soto shop, or he came over. I told him on the phone about my win.

"We should play as partners," he suggested.

"I can't do that. It's bad enough that I'm taking the risk. What if we both have a streak of bad luck?"

"If one of us has a bad streak, maybe the other will win."

"Look, I owe you for turning me on to Vegas," I said. "If I win again, I'll toss you something."

"Stay positive," Mike said.

There was a check cashing place about a mile up Brooklyn Avenue. I don't know what I was thinking, but I drove up there with a blank check. There were three windows but only one attendant when I got there. I dropped my business card on the window slot that divided customers from clerks. It was a busy place.

The sleepy-eyed blonde at the window picked up my card.

"I'd like to speak to the manager."

The girl brought him to the window beside her. I tried sizing him up. He was probably in his forties, with light brown hair, sideburns, and thick black glasses. The suit he wore was nothing special.

"Come on in," he said. "Walk to that door. I'll buzz you in."

He introduced himself as Rene, the owner.

"No doubt about it. You have a gold mine going for you," he said. "I drive by there every day on my way home."

"Thanks," I said. "I want to set up something with you when I need cash. You can cash a check for me?"

He smiled like I had made a joke. "That's what we do," he said. "How much?"

"Right now, I'd like five thousand."

I didn't mention Vegas.

"Five costs you thirty dollars, but since we're neighbors, twenty dollars."

"Cool," I said. "Rene, I cash a lot of checks with Chester at the gas station next to me. He always has a long line, but if you want to call him, he'll tell you I'm solid."

"No need," he said.

I took the check out of my pocket. "Should I make it payable to myself?"

Rene nodded.

I used my own pen to fill out the check at his desk.

"Perfect," Rene said, glancing over it. "I'll get you the money."

He handed me the money in an envelope.

"If you need anything from me," I said, "just raise your hand. We do great paint and bodywork."

"I know," he said. "One of my morning girls got her car painted there. It looks brand new."

I had the envelope in my hands and felt excitement and misgiving at the same time. I put it in my pocket. I could have gotten the five thousand from Chester. Chester would have held the check. Rene was not going to hold the check. He would probably deposit it on Monday since it was already late Friday. Even if he deposited the check that day, my check wouldn't get to my bank until Wednesday. By then, I would be back from Vegas to deposit the money to cover the check. I was thinking like I'd come back a winner again.

"I saw you drive away," Elena said. "Did you go do a quickie somewhere?"

I told her what I did.

"What if you lose?"

I did the sign of the cross again.

"Don't say that."

Elena wasn't alone when she dropped me off at the airport for the eight pm flight out of LAX. Susie was with her. Susie kept a stream of bright chatter going the whole way there. I got out on the sidewalk with my carry-on and leaned into my open door.

From behind the wheel, Elena blew me a kiss. Susie got out of the back and climbed into the front seat.

"I'll keep your seat warm for you, G," Susie said, giving me a peck.

"Are you two going to do nasty stuff tonight?"

"Big time," Susie said.

Elena only laughed.

On my past trips, I never gambled on the night I arrived. I waited until Saturday. Waiting was Mike's idea. He said you have to come to the table calm. You can't be calm if you just arrived.

I dropped all of the five thousand that night. I flew back on Saturday morning. I was at the shop before noon. I wasn't supposed to be back until Sunday. Elena saw me and frowned. Susie saw me and smiled.

I got out of the taxi. Elena walked up and hugged me, then we walked to the shop holding hands. She had a worried look about her but didn't ask. Up in the office behind closed doors, I called Mike and told him what I lost.

"Hey, you won twenty-five hundred and nine thousand. You gave them back some of their money."

He was right, but what did that matter? I had put the money into the business. It wasn't like I'd stockpiled the winnings or took cash from savings to go back. The loss hurt. I should have let it end there.

On Tuesday, I got five thousand from Chester and deposited it into my account. I checked my balance. The check I'd cashed had not come in yet. Wednesday, I called the bank to find out my balance. The check to Rene didn't clear until Thursday. For twenty dollars, I'd had five thousand to use for one week, minus a day.

Elena could go with me the following weekend. She drove us there. I had five thousand in my pocket, proceeds from a check from my new friend, Rene's Check Cashing Service.

ALL THE SEATS at the table are taken, so Elena stands behind me. I play twenty-dollar hands[1] and always double down when the dealer shows a low card. I am losing.

I count out two thousand and put it on the table.

"Money plays," I say to the dealer. The dealer repeats that to the pit boss, who nods his approval. The dealer busts and pays me with chips. I pocket the cash and let the two thousand in chips ride.

The dealer shows a high card. I had twelve.

I had the dealer hit me. A beautiful nine comes up.

The dealer has twenty.

I win.

Elena pats my shoulder.

I leave the four thousand to play. The chairs are already full, and their occupants are getting noisy. Some gawkers make their way to the table, watching and yelling at the action. People are looking now. My eyes are on my two cards, twelve. The dealer shows a jack. I try to appear calm, but my heart is a freight train.

I ask for a card. I get a seven.

The dealer shows twelve. Hits. Gets a king. He busts.

The pile on the table is getting big. Eight thousand in chips. I turn to look at Elena. We lock eyes, the two of us a thing apart from all the noise and casino craziness. The air conditioning is blasting, and little beads of sweat stand on her forehead.

"Ride," she whispers.

---

1. Adjusted for inflation, $20.00 in 1962 is equal to $171.32 in 2020.

I turn back to the table and meet the dealer's eyes. I tap the pile. Take a deep breath. I feel the onlookers watching. I feel Elena at my back.

"Play it all."

My hand is a blackjack.

I push with the dealer. He has a blackjack, too. I have a chance to pull out.

I let it ride again.

I feel Elena tapping my back. She's actually trembling.

Dealer busts.

When I say ride, the dealer calls the pit boss to approve the play. It takes three seconds.

The table is hot. Every seat is full. Spectators are more than a row deep, but I'm not watching them. I'm watching the chips, the cards, feeling Elena behind me.

We take sixty-five thousand dollars home. Oh my, that was so much money in the sixties.

I WAS COMPED from the regular room to a beautiful suite. We took in a show.

We took advantage of the free food, the suite, and the bed.

WE RETURNED from the show and went back to our suite, the air still electric with the thrill of the evening. I was buzzing with excitement, my words tumbling out as I made plans for the future. Elena, with a sultry smile, began to undress, her movements slow and deliberate, each piece of clothing falling to the floor like a whisper.

I sank onto a plush, gold fabric ottoman, the rich texture cool against my skin as I slipped off my shoes. The room was a symphony of opulence, from the crystal chandeliers casting a warm, golden glow to the velvet drapes that framed the panoramic view of the city below.

"I owe Chester five for the loss last week. I have to cover the five that Rene gave me to come up here. That leaves fifty-five thousand. I need to give Mike two thousand," I said, my mind racing with numbers and obligations.

"A thousand to Mike is a lot of bread. Why two?" Elena asked, her voice a husky murmur as she stood there, completely naked, her body a vision of curves and shadows in the dim light.

"Why not? I told him I'd take care of him on my next big win," I replied, my eyes tracing the lines of her body. "The balance is going to carry us without floating for more than two months."

"Fantastic," Elena said, her tone dripping with satisfaction. She moved closer, her skin brushing against mine, sending shivers down my spine. She yanked me towards her, silencing my rambling with a look that spoke volumes.

My clothes joined Elena's on the floor, a tangled mess of fabric and desire. We moved the discussion to the bed, the sheets cool and inviting against our heated skin.

"Now I know how a lottery winner feels," I said, my voice a low rumble as I took in the suite. It was larger than my apartment, every inch of it dripping with luxury, and an army of hotel employees ready to cater to our every whim with just a phone call.

"We don't have a lottery in California," Elena whispered, her breath hot against my ear.

"They do in Mexico," I replied, my voice trailing off as her hands cupped my cheeks, turning my face to hers until our lips were almost touching.

"Do I need to sit on your face?" she asked, her eyes dark with desire.

I stopped talking, my breath catching in my throat. "Been a

long time since you did that," I said, my voice barely more than a whisper. She had my full attention now, every nerve ending alive with anticipation.

I did not go back to a blackjack table or a slot machine that night. Instead, I lost myself in Elena, in the heat of her skin, the taste of her lips, and the intoxicating scent of her hair. The world outside ceased to exist, and for that moment, we were the only two people in the universe.

On Monday morning, I shared my good fortune. I gave Mike a thousand dollars, and he flipped out.

"I'm going to Vegas this coming weekend," he said gleefully.

"You're a big boy," I said.

I tried to give Elena five thousand. She gave me a hard time.

"I got nothing coming. But I love you all the more for offering."

Eventually, I got her to accept a thousand.

I gave each employee two hundred dollars in cash, except for Susie. I gave Susie five hundred on the sly, but she told Elena anyway.

"Please stop giving the money away," Elena said. "Put it in the bank."

I kept two thousand for my pocket. I deposited the Vegas money in the bank along with the weekend income from both shops in the company account. Depositing over ten thousand in cash was no big deal back then. It became a big deal in 1970 under the Bank Secrecy Act.

When my accountant came by to do the books, I told him where the money had come from. His eyebrows went up, and he smiled.

"I'll work it out," he said. "You need to tell me how much you lost before you won. There are taxes to deal with. We don't need to do it today."

"Taxes, are you kidding me?"

"Uncle Sam needs to get his. Like I said. I'll work it out."

When he left that day, things were different. Chester was holding no checks. All bills were paid, including taxes. More than twenty-seven thousand was sitting in the checking account. I'd never seen such blue skies. It was a huge relief to be out from under all the pressure.

Mike went to Vegas that weekend. Elena and I went to bed.

We were in and out of bed from Friday night to Sunday morning. My thoughts were clear. I was on track. The pressure was not over because insurance companies still owed me a bunch of money. I should have cut insurance work that day and settled for the car painting business that was supporting everything. The Soto shop was not even breaking even. Mike was there, and he was getting five cars painted a day. I had hoped for more, but I was wrong. Maybe the huge Sears building overpowered my shop right next door. I was afraid to stop advertising with Pepe because I felt it would totally kill the business we were getting. I kept paying the radio station. Money goes fast.

Judge Black referred a bail bondsman named Luca.

"Any friend of Judge Black's is a friend of mine," I said, shaking Luca's hand when he brought in his car.

Luca's office was across the street from the ELA Courthouse, where Judge Black presided. I painted Luca's car, then his wife's car, then his two daughters' cars. Luca introduced me to Judge Garcia and Judge Munoz, both on the bench in Judge Black's courthouse.

I never accepted any money for the work I did for the judges.

My cash flow struggles were not due to the little bit of free work I did but rather stemmed from the erratic payments from insurance companies. Payments only arrived sporadically, determined by when they sent a check. It was clear that the profit margins on large insurance invoices were much higher than those on simple paint jobs. Although I frequently expressed my readiness to move away from insurance work, letting go proved to be challenging. Insurance adjusters kept sending me more customers.

It was midweek, a highlight in what had been one of our best weeks ever, yet Elena wore a frown. We sat at our kitchen table, enjoying the rich aroma of pastrami sandwiches from The Hat, the warm, savory scent filling the air and making my mouth water. As she approached the kitchen trash bin, she tilted it toward me, revealing two empty Canadian Club bottles balanced on top.

"I'm not comfortable with this, G. We're drinking every day after work. Doesn't it remind you of Ramirez?"

Ramirez sold me the body shop on Brooklyn & Rowan. He drank every day, as if each hour dragged on, weighing heavily until 5 PM arrived—that's when he popped open a new bottle of whisky.

"Ramirez drank at the shop; we drink at home. It's part of relaxing after work," I said.

"It's a terrible habit." Elena was calm but firm. "When I returned from Hawaii, I was so accustomed to overindulging that I just continued it here until I got that DUI. After that, I mostly cut back," she said, glancing at the trash. "Or maybe I was just lying to myself."

"I'm never going to drink more than one drink and drive," I replied firmly. "You know that."

Elena took a bite of her sandwich, chewing thoughtfully

before speaking. "Let's not drink every day. It's not good for us. It turns our morning jog into a farce, leaving us to sweat out alcohol instead of water."

"I dig the way you communicate," I said. "Are you saying we need to give up booze entirely?"

"Let's do two drinks limit per day, no exceptions," she suggested, blotting her lips with a napkin. "Are you in or not?"

"I'm in, two drinks, no more," I said. "How about sex?"

"Sex, yes, every day."

"Not true. There's at least a week when we can't."

"We could," Elena said. "But you don't want to."

"Oh, baby, that's gross," I said.

She laughed.

"How about Susie?" I asked.

She showed me a tiny smirk. "That ex of yours and the other girl got you addicted to three on a bed."

"No pressure, baby. My hands are full with just you."

"Then why do you want Susie?"

"I don't want Susie."

"You do," she said.

After a pause, I said, "I like living in the moment, and so do you. Come on, cop out, I'm right, right?"

She grew thoughtful. "I get this guilt trip about it."

"No problem, we don't have to do it anymore. I'm cool with that."

"Okay, we can do Susie things, but we have a deal, two drinks maximum per day." Then she sighed and said, "We should do weed. We could stop the drinking altogether."

"I can't inhale," I said.

"I'll teach you," she said and put her hands on me. We were finished eating; she was on her feet and positioned behind me. I was still sitting.

"Two drinks limit is better," I said. "Weed equals jail."

"People don't get jail for smoking weed."

"Baby, where have you been?" I said. "Weed is illegal."

"Okay. Two drinks, G."

"Deal," I said.

12

EASTLAND KEEPS GROWING

Paulo was an upholsterer who worked at a shop on Olympic Boulevard, but his bosses there would not give him bonuses or anything other than his paycheck. He had years of experience doing car upholstery and showed me his car interior, leather, tuck and roll, beautiful work, exactly what was trending in the sixties. Paulo wanted room to grow his job. He came aboard knowing precisely what he needed: a spot to work, a jump start of money to stock rolls of display fabric, a sewing machine, and a few other things. He said a thousand dollars would cover it all. On each job, he would give me back sixty percent minus the cost of materials. On display, he had fabric, leather, convertible top material, things like that. He wanted a draw of two hundred dollars weekly until he started pulling money in.

I gave him the two car stalls right under the office stairs, not dead space, but only used when cars were being moved around. It was a good place for a trimmer like Paulo to work.

Elena liked Paulo. He was thirty or so, very suave, and gave off a kind of a con man vibe. Who am I to talk smack about that?

I'm the guy who got Thelma to give me thirty-five hundred dollars when I was only fifteen.

Elena said, "The only part I don't like is the two hundred a week. I don't think he needed a thousand to get it going. It will be totally cool as long as it only costs you his draw and not for long. We have a body shop, paint shop, mechanic shop, and upholstery shop with him. That's full service.

"I love it," I said, matching her excitement. "I'm not fronting any big money; if he gets a job and doesn't have the bucks to buy the material, I'll give it to him. He'll give it back when he gets paid, same as when we started with Jose."

Jose's department was now part of Eastland. All his jobs were written up on our invoices. Our split was the same, but Jose was no longer collecting directly from customers. My attorney,

Carlos, explained liability concerns in letting Jose continue on a cash basis while working under my roof. If a customer claimed a brake job done by Jose caused an accident, I couldn't explain why there was no Eastland invoice. By invoicing through Eastland, I had liability insurance.

It took Paulo about three weeks to quit his job and build a large worktable made with tall posts where he hung materials to display for clients. When a customer came in for a paint job, most times they did some bodywork, and sometimes they wanted new seat covers or an entire interior redone, depending on the car's age. I made it a point to be around as much as possible when he bid on a job and put a job together. Paulo had a special of fifty dollars for redoing the front and back seats in leather. Depending on the make of the car, he did that in about an hour. It seldom ended up doing only the seats. The door panels were extra. The ceiling fabric was extra. Everything was extra. It was not long before he had more work than he could handle. He brought in his brother Alex to work with him. I had to buy another sewing machine.

REWIND A BIT. I forgot to mention Mike going to Las Vegas after I gave him the thousand. He drove there with his fiancée Vicki. When he got back, he claimed he'd only lost half of the thousand. "You have miraculous luck," Mike said. "Touch me and give me some of that luck." He grinned, and we shook hands.

"Nothing lasts forever," I said. "That time, I lost five thousand; it was their money, but it hurt to lose it."

"Can't gamble with fright of losing," he said. "Remember that when you go back." He had looked back toward his car, where Vicki was sleeping in the passenger seat. "We haven't even gone home yet," he said, then headed for his car.

When he was out of earshot, Elena said, "No Vegas for a while, please. Stay a winner."

We were on the shop floor, waiting for customers to pick up their finished cars an hour before closing time.

"No plans to go for now," I said.

Elena hugged me with such enthusiasm I still remember.

Susie had just delivered a car and walked up to us. "I'd like some of that."

"What are you doing tomorrow night?" Elena asked.

"I'm game for anything," Susie said.

"Hey, that's my line," I said.

"I stole your line during one of those moments."

"Shh," Elena said, laughing. "Not so loud."

Selena[1] and I had opened the ice cream parlor and worked shoulder-to-shoulder from early morning until closing time. Now, it was Elena with me all the time, just as Selena was back then.

I was paying Selena a hundred a week, more than twice minimum wage, but if I actually counted the hours that she worked with me at the shop, she was working for peanuts. There was a vast disparity. I was giving the upholstery guy two hundred a week and his brother one hundred. Elena should have been making more money. Looking back, I find it hard to understand why I didn't fix that and give her what she deserved.

---

1. Selena was my first wife. We were married when I was 17 years old. I went AWOL from the Navy, and we settled down in Juarez, Mexico, where we opened an ice cream parlor.

I couldn't tell how much time had passed, but it hadn't been long since my last trip to Vegas. Gil was at the main shop, and Susie, Elena, and I were all busy. The buzz of activity at that shop was a genuine blessing; we were always in motion.

"Are you sure you want to do this?" Elena asked as we sat in my office. The louvers were open, allowing us to see and hear the bustling hive of activity below.

"It's just a quick trip. My exposure is five thousand, not a dime more," I replied.

"G, it's your money. No explanation needed." She embraced me. "I've got to get back to the floor."

I was finishing up some tasks at my desk when Elena reached the door. She turned back, giving me a playful look over her shoulder and a wink. "We could have some fun with Susie if you decide to stay."

I looked up, shaking my head with a smile. "You are so mean."

"We could gang up on you," she teased, still standing at the door, ready to leave. I blew her a kiss; my mind was made up. Vegas was calling me.

I passed on the nasty. I took a taxi to LAX because I had an afternoon flight. I flew up and broke Mike's rule that you don't gamble when you arrive but wait until the next day.

I was surprised I got a king-sized, sleek, modern, and fully comped room on the top floor. They remember the dummies who gamble. I immediately went down to the casino. I was not calm, cool, and collected like Mike said to be. In less than two hours, I lost the five thousand. It was the second time I lost five thousand, fast. I thought of my accountant about my losses to offset the wins. I wasn't in Las Vegas looking for tax write-offs!

I called the shop, and it rang. I checked my watch. It was after hours, so I called my apartment. Elena answered. She was at my apartment.

"Come home," she said. "You're still ahead."

I didn't have to think twice about it; I wanted Elena to Western Union me two thousand from the office cash. She was such a trooper—no arguments or hesitation on her part. I may be mistaken, but I don't recall ever having a disagreement with her. If she had pushed back about the money, I'm sure I would have had something to say. But I was wound up, on edge, and starting to feel the sickness that comes from the urge to gamble.

Elena didn't send the money by Western Union. On Saturday, she dropped Susie off at Eastland and headed to Las Vegas. A little after eleven in the morning, she was in my fancy, modern, comped bed.

"I'm sorry you drove all the way up here," I said.

"You're not sorry," she pushed me back lightly. "Let me check the bedding."

She shook around the sheets. It didn't take two minutes for us to jump in bed.

"I should shower," she said after the first time. "I'm sweaty from the drive. It was so hot the air-conditioning couldn't keep it cool until I hit the state line."

I touched her.

"No shower. I want you sweaty and smelly."

"I'm not smelly," she said. "I showered before I left."

"Did Susie shower with you?"

By the time she said no, I was inside her.

WE USED the free tickets they gave me to go to the brunch buffet, a gimmick to keep you from venturing out of the hotel.

Blackjack tables had single decks. Mike counted cards. Maybe I could learn to do that, but I don't think it helps you win, and if the guy above watching the table concludes you are counting cards, you get kicked out. I never saw that happen, but that's Blackjack, according to Mike.

Of the two thousand Elena brought me, a thousand were in twenties and tens. Counting them out, I felt like I had broken into my piggy bank. I bought two hundred dollars in twenty-dollar chips.

Every time the dealer showed a small card, I doubled down. In other words, if I was playing forty dollars, I'd raise my bet by another forty.

I was not a card counter, but I had no problem tracking my wins and losses—not to the penny, but close, especially when stone-cold sober. I figured I was winning a little.

Unless a table was terrible, I didn't move. That's advice from Mike, who believed a cold table would turn, and so the strategy was to lower your bets until there's a change.

At first, Elena sat next to me. She was not playing. It's okay to take up a vacant seat until the seat is needed. I like to play when the table is full. With a full table, the dealer shuffles much more often. Eventually, she got up and stood behind me.

"Change color," I said to the dealer, pushing three thousand in twenty-dollar chips that had accumulated.

"Color change," the dealer said aloud for the pit boss, who didn't even look and repeated it. Mike had said they did that for the spies looking through the mirrored ceiling tiles.

The dealer exchanged thirty-one-hundred-dollar chips for the twenties.

I turned around to see Elena, there with a face of patience and a smile. I had to write this to realize how much Elena meant to me at the time. She was a life jacket that kept me from drowning, a cane that kept me from falling over my own feet, and crutches to help me walk after I fucked-up.

I put ten hundred-dollar chips to play.[2]

I busted.

I repeated the thousand-dollar bet.

The dealer showed a deuce.

To double down, I had to put up the thousand I had in a hundred chips.

Dealer busted.

Not counting my small chips, I had four thousand.

I thought of Mike and the word fright.

I pushed the four thousand in chips forward. There were some oohs from around the table, but not from Elena.

I got a blackjack. I heard a whole host of noises and reactions, and in it, I heard Elena do a little squeal. The dealer stayed at seventeen.

I could have walked with ten thousand. That would have meant I earned back the five I lost when I called Elena. With ten, I could pay back the shop safe and be a three thousand winner. I didn't consult with Elena in front of all the people.

I liked it when I had green cash and played big hands by letting cash play, but my money was all in chips. I let the ten-thousand ride. The pit boss gave the table a thumbs-up and walked away.

I CONVERTED my chips to cash at the cashier, a pretty, heavily made-up girl who counted out seventy-thousand three hundred[3] dollars. I gave her a hundred-dollar bill. I also gave the dealer four tips totaling four hundred dollars.

A bellman moved the few things I had in my room to

---

2. $1,000 then is $8,500 in 2020
3. $70,300 then is $594.252 in 2020

another, bigger suite. I gave him a twenty, and he freaked out. We opened the door to a room of gilt French antiques. We sat in the living room and drank from a complimentary bottle of champagne. I never liked it, and I don't think Elena liked it, but I opened it, and we each had a glass. The gorgeous French sofa was a totally different style from the first suite, old fashioned and stuffy, but beautiful like something in a department store window that you were only meant to look at, not touch, not sit on it as we were doing.

So, we sat on that couch and sipped champagne, and it was the first time I saw Elena cry.

"Baby don't cry. If you hadn't come, I'd have gone home a loser. If you had sent me the money by Western Union, I would have lost it. *You* are the reason I won."

That made her cry even more.

She shaded her brow with her hand as if that would keep me from seeing.

"Never mind me. I'm blowing off the stress that built up standing behind you."

"Did you at least cum?"

She whacked me.

"No, I didn't cum."

We were completely worn out from the weight of our stress. In the midst of it all, we found solace in each other, embracing tightly, our arms wrapping around one another as if to shield ourselves from the chaos of the casino where we'd been. We exchanged soft kisses, each one a gentle reminder of our connection. Our words fell into whispers, delicate and intimate as if we were sharing secrets meant only for our ears—like lovers sharing tender confessions in the quiet of the night. In those moments, time seemed to stand still, and the world outside faded as we lost ourselves in the warmth of our affection.

IN THE MORNING, we had brunch, passed the casino without stopping, and went straight to the valet. I drove. When it got hot going up the mountain range, I turned off the air-conditioning as recommended by the signs. We breezed through the desert on a two-lane highway that had a reputation as a car- and people-killer. The windows were open, and Elena's panties were in her purse for the same reason: cross-ventilation.

"It's hot," Elena said and put her bare feet on the dashboard.

"The truckers are getting a peep show," I said.

A well-timed gust of wind blew her skirt up practically over her head. We roared in laughter. She roared first, and I laughed because her laughter was so funny. The truck driver put in his five cents' worth. As we passed him, he sounded his air horn.

More laughter.

"I didn't know you flashed," I said, remembering Selena.

"I didn't know either," she giggled. "G, don't be chicken. Pull over. I want it now."

I didn't do it, but we laughed for hours.

When we got to the apartment, our voices were hoarse. I was so happy I didn't know how to control myself. It was Sunday. Elena stashed her purse with the seventy thousand dollars in it under my mattress, and we each took a shower. Twenty-four hours had passed since I won.

∽

I DIDN'T VISIT my daughter enough. That started when Sophia told me to call to let her know I wanted to come over. That's my excuse. I should not have felt I needed a reason to visit, but Vegas gave me a reason.

From the Vegas haul, I gave Sophia two thousand dollars. She resisted a little.

"I'm okay with what you are sending every month. I'm doing okay."

"Good. You are doing okay, but I want you to have this."

"Your body shops must be doing good," she said.

"Absolutely," I said.

I never told her it was Las Vegas.

GIL AND SUSIE handled the floor while Elena and I had lunch in the office. Mike was working the Soto shop alone, but he called Alexa to drive over from Eastland II if he got overwhelmed. I think he called her over so they could fool around. I never asked him. Alexa was my age, a looker. But then, I think all women are lookers, whatever size they are. I've always loved ladies.

AS I GAZED AT ELENA, I could tell she had something weighing on her mind. We sat on the restaurant patio, surrounded by the warm scent of sizzling tacos and the gentle hum of conversation from nearby tables. The sun beat down on us, but the shade of the umbrella above and the occasional breeze from the outdoor ceiling fan kept us cool. The wooden baskets in front of us were filled with an assortment of colorful tacos, each one carefully crafted with fresh ingredients and savory spices.

Elena's eyes sparkled as she dipped the tip of her taco into a creamy dollop of guacamole, the sound of the crunchy shell giving way to the soft avocado filling. "I try not to influence you," she said, her voice low and husky as she chewed.

I took a bite of my own taco, savoring the combination of flavors and textures - the crispy shell, the tender beef, and the tangy slaw. "Tell me what you have in mind," I said, my mouth still full as I gestured for her to continue.

Elena's brow furrowed in concern as she began to speak. "You don't need to do insurance work. You do a fifteen-hundred-dollar job, and by the time you cover parts, paint, and labor, I doubt you make twenty-five percent profit. And then, to add insult to injury, you have to wait to get paid." She shook her head, her dark hair rustling in the breeze. "And then there are the check cashing fees you pay when floating checks to cover shortages."

While I admired Elena's passion and conviction, it felt like she was preaching to the choir. I was acutely aware of the financial pressures that came with waiting for insurance checks—repairing cars for clients insured by the insurance company meant big-ticket items, but payment was often delayed. In fact, only Farmers Insurance paid me upon completion of the repairs. I would rely on a check-cashing place that knew me well; they provided cash for my checks without depositing them until I instructed. During that hold period, I would deposit the cash into my business account to cover outstanding checks, albeit at a fee. Even now, the memory of that precarious juggling act twists my stomach into knots.

"Are you saying that maybe we should only focus on Farmers Insurance because they pay upon completion?" I asked, already knowing the answer.

"Exactly," Elena replied firmly. "While we haven't run all the numbers yet, my rough estimate is they owe around forty thousand dollars." Her voice was low and serious, and I could feel the weight of her words settling between us.

The sound of her voice seemed louder than it needed to be, given our proximity, and her softly spoken words hung heavy in the air. I nodded thoughtfully, knowing I wasn't going to cut off the insurance work.

"I'll think about it," I said finally, pushing my chair back from the table. As our meal concluded, we got up, leaving behind empty wooden baskets, and headed out into the warm sunshine.

∽

I PREFERRED to reward my team with tips and bonuses for working late or for exceptional performance, but I noticed my payroll consistently swelled every time I returned from Vegas as a winner. Mike often mentioned missing calls while he was busy writing estimates or talking to customers. I suggested he hire someone to handle the office work, with Elena training her on the paperwork—a somewhat weak move given that the shop wasn't breaking even. It was easy to overlook such details when I was flush with cash from Nevada.

I had always envisioned our shop being spick and span, so I hired a couple whose cleaning skills transformed the place. I often wondered how we managed before them; they kept my office and the entire shop spotless, including the floors. Jose spread sawdust in the mechanic area, and the couple would sweep it up, along with any grease or oil.

In addition to cleaning, I made a few shop improvements I had wanted to pursue earlier but couldn't afford. I invested in new illuminated signs for our already busy shop. I even offered Elena my Impala, but when she declined, I traded it in for a new convertible Impala and paid the difference in cash.

13

OH NO, ANOTHER EASTLAND

So, I had my new car. I drove it to the car wash and noticed a "For Lease" sign on the adjoining building.

I made some inquiries. The car wash owner said he washed more cars in a day than some local car washes do in a week.

"You put a paint shop there, and you will be swarmed with customers," he said, "because of the high volume I do here."

I felt that familiar feeling about the building. Before the sunset that day, I had signed a lease. I was gone all day and never called the shop.

Elena was very testy.

"You cannot imagine how worried I was," she said. "Didn't you have a dime to call?"

I told her what I'd done.

She sighed.

I knew she wanted to urge me to be cautious or something like that. The shop bills had been so problematic, and now everything was running so smoothly. Why would I rock the boat when everything was going so smoothly? But she didn't say that because it was something that we both knew.

Now there was another shop, an Eastland IV. After closing time, I drove us there to show it off. I had the keys.

"What was this? I don't remember?" she asked.

"It was a tire shop. I don't remember it either."

I turned on the lights, and we walked around. There wasn't much there. A sturdy old desk in the little bit of an office, nothing of a waiting room, a metal table, and a couple of chairs. Compared to how Eastland had been, it was clean. It could use a paint job and some spiffing up.

We stood there in silence. Maybe not actual silence. We weren't talking, but we could hear the random bumps and squeaks and creaks of an empty building and the echoes of traffic, a police car or ambulance, and a noisy motorcycle screaming down the busy boulevard.

"It's a perfect size. The rent is five hundred a month for the first year and a twenty percent increase for four years. In the fifth year, we renegotiate."

"You did this in one day? Gosh."

"Baby, tell me you like it." The lights inside were easily bright enough for me to see her face, but her expression was inscrutable.

"There's only room to do five cars a day," she said, looking around.

"I thought the same thing. I can put Gil here, a bodyman and a painter. Maybe a painter's helper."

"For sure, you need a painter's helper," she said.

"Holmberg will spring for the spray booth, oven, and compressor."

"Did you tell him?"

"Not yet. I'm sorry I didn't tell you, but it happened fast. The owner of the car wash called the landlord. He came right over.

We bought the lease forms and sat right here," I pulled out one of the metal chairs, and it screeched against the concrete floor, "and we worked out the terms."

I recalled how Mrs. Goldberg had marked up the form from Walcott's Stationary, that became the master lease I had on the main shop, Eastland I, the cow. I had learned a lot following Mrs. Goldberg around.

"Amazing," Elena said. "What do you figure it'll cost to fix it up?"

We sauntered across the floor toward the office.

"The signs alone will be a thousand. New light fixtures, paint, waiting room buildout, fixing up the office, another two thousand."

"Better get the boys over here to fix it up. I'm thinking it's going to cost more." Elena said.

I thought I heard some excitement in her voice. That was more like it.

"Tomorrow, I'll call on the spray booth and oven and go from there."

"Okay," Elena said, wiping off a pane of glass with her hand and looking out.

"I got the owner to kick in three months free rent while I fix it up."

That made Elena turn from the glass looking surprised, then she broke out laughing. "You always got an angle. How did you finagle that? That's a steal."

Her approval was a boost. "I figure, less than two months, and we can open it up."

Elena nodded her head vaguely in the direction of the car wash.

"The car wash customers wait for their cars twenty feet from the shop entrance. That's good."

"You like?"

"I like."

She gave me that look.

"Wait here one second," I said.

I closed the front doors, and we did it on the old desk that had nothing on top of it. It was not a quickie.

∼

HE WAS A BUSY MAN, but I never had to make an appointment to see him. Holmberg said, "I have no problem loaning money for equipment because the bank looks at it as a collateralized loan, even though it's not like having a pink slip on a car. But slow down, George."

"It's too late," I said. "I'm already in this." I leaned forward in my chair. Holmberg's office had gotten bigger over the years, but he hadn't changed much.

"I'm referring to the next shop. Work on building your bank balances. Cash talks." Holmberg smiled.

"If I didn't have the receivables from insurance companies, I'd have seventy thousand in the bank on top of what I have now."

"It could be you need to slow down the insurance work or the expansion so that you can handle the receivables without it strangling you. You don't want to end up overextended."

He was right, but I had just rented another shop.

I wanted to be the kind of man who never has to look back and regret a decision. There's no question that I've had sick moments when I didn't think. Sometimes I'm a leap-first look-later kind of guy.

Mr. Holmberg reached over and shook my hand as he got up.

"Slow accumulation of wealth works, son. Don't rush it."

∼

As if I were my own contractor, I called my sandblasting guy, who liked to moonlight, my electrician, painter, and sign painter. The spray booth company and the oven company joined forces and went right to drawing out plans and checking on city permits.

My mechanic Jose went to see it. He loved it because it still had three hydraulic lifts that the tire shop used. I had no use for them and no room for Jose to do mechanic work over there, so I told him to chill and be happy where he was.

The Soto shop where Mike worked was very close. He came by to take a look. Mike wore t-shirts and jeans like I did, but he had at least seventeen-inch biceps. He liked the new shop. We walked through the shop, then went over to the desk to sit down.

"Let Gil take over Soto and let me work the new place."

"You got it," I said.

He got in a bodybuilder pose and said, "I'll flex at the ladies waiting for their cars to be washed and get them to come over for a paint job."

"Good idea," I said. "No matter how many housewives you dazzle, the problem is that here is going to be like Soto. I don't think you can paint more than five cars a day. It's too small."

"I'll work it," he said. "I'll work it out."

I had a great deal of confidence in Mike, almost as much as he had in himself.

I wanted more than feedback about the new shop. I had taken in Mr. Holmberg's suggestions and realized I might end up in a bind. I wanted to be ready if that point came.

Mike knew Chester gave me cash when I needed it and held the checks until I had the money to cover them. I also told him about Rene, though I never asked Rene to hold the check.

"It takes four or more days to hit the bank after he deposits," I told Mike.

"I'm not a numbers guy. Just tell me what you want done. I know you want something." He grinned.

"Find two or more check cashing places to have just in case we need cash on a float."

"What's a float?"

"Mike, I just told you. It takes four days or more for a check to get to my bank after the check cashing place deposits the check. The time that it is just hanging there, that's a float. It gives me time to cover the check you cash. Right now, we're good."

"I understand," he said. "No sweat. I'll poke around."

JOSE WAS DOING VERY WELL. He had a helper that he paid from the percentage he kept from each job. Eagle Auto Parts, where he bought his parts, was a huge place a mile west of the main shop. The company sold new parts and rebuilt everything under the hood of a car that can be rebuilt carburetors, starters, water pumps, radiators, to name a few. Jose would call for parts, and no matter how small the order, the parts were delivered in less than an hour. The owner of the company was Sam Rabin, whom I'd never met. Sam called me on the phone to invite me to breakfast at six-thirty in the morning, my jogging time. I accepted out of curiosity.

When she heard about the breakfast, Susie told Elena and me that Sam had a bunch of companies at the Eagle Parts location. Sam financed cars for the employees of his customers. For example, if Susie wanted to buy a used car, Sam would finance the car for Susie because she worked for us, and we were his customer.

As soon as I made the appointment, I complained about missing jogging.

"Pretend to yourself you're in Vegas and couldn't jog," Elena teased.

"You'll have to skip, too," I said. "We have one car."

"I can stay at my aunt's tonight," she said. "I haven't seen my aunt in ages."

"So, what do I do at home? I don't have a dog or a cat."

"You have your fish," she laughed.

After moving back to the apartment complex, I installed a double aquarium in the living room filled with beautiful tropical fish. At first, I did the maintenance myself, which meant removing and washing the filter system and panning the rock at the bottom. But going into business for myself took a bite out of my time. At the cleaners where I dropped off my laundry, I found a card on the bulletin board, a school kid who did aquarium maintenance. He came once a week, my aquarium was crystal clear, and my fish families were happy campers. All I had to do is feed them. They'd swim up high and allow me to pet them.

I hadn't been alone in my apartment since Olivia.

"You really don't want to come home?"

"You need to be with Sam at six-thirty," Elena said. "You need to leave the house at six. You should have told him lunch."

"I should have, but I didn't."

"Okay, do what you want," Elena said and gave me a look. It wasn't a mean look, but it stung a little.

I asked Mike to come over at closing time so we could teach him how to prepare the daily deposit. I wanted him to prepare the new store's deposit so that I didn't have to mess with it. We'd work out how I would get the prepared deposit each day, or maybe he could make the deposit himself. He was going to be working the office alone. Gil at Soto Street had a secretary, Lucy, to answer the phone, organize sales invoices for the accountant, and do the deposits.

At a little after six, Mike arrived, and we shut the doors. "G, head home," Elena said. "Susie and I will close. I'll teach Mike the deposit routine."

"I can learn anything," he said cheerfully.

He was almost too cheerful. If I had declined and not gone home, I thought it would look as though I didn't trust leaving Mike and Elena together.

I kissed Elena, pecked Susie, and before I left, stopped in the market to say hi to Jesse and Chris. Those guys were always there.

"Get a life," I teased them.

"Look who's talking," Chris said.

Jesse laughed and gave me a thumbs-up. He was cooler than Chris, but I loved them both.

As I opened the door to my car, I saw Susie pull the accordion gate shut and put the padlock in place. She had her own set of keys for everything. Some days she closed. Some days she opened.

"Where's Elena?"

She walked over, looking at me with surprise.

"They're upstairs. She's giving a class to Mike. I thought you were gone, Jefe."

"I stopped at the market to say hi. Where are you off to?"

"Same old same old. Crossing the street to catch the streetcar for home."

I opened my car door for her. She was six feet away. "I'll drive you."

We stood there.

"Are you sure?"

"Come on," I said. "No big deal."

She got in the front seat. We headed down Rowan past Elena's aunt's house, then took First Street West, my old hunting grounds.

"Tell me when to turn," I said.

"Keep going."

"How come Elena's not going home with you tonight?" she asked.

"I have to see Sam early in the morning. I have no clue what he wants," I told Susie. "Have you ever met him?"

"Never. I don't think he gets out much. I heard he gets there early and leaves when everything shuts down."

She pointed out her house as I slowed. It was getting dark. No bars on her windows. Nice iron door in front of a wood door. It was a cute bungalow, and I told her so.

"Want to come in?"

I turned to look at her. I don't think there was any part of Susie's anatomy I had not visited. I had a flash of her body on me and my body on hers, a replay, not fantasy. It wasn't like we'd never had sex before, but we'd never been alone together. Elena had been right there in bed with us.

"Park the car, Jefe. I got a nice place, small but cozy. I'll make us something to eat."

I parked along the curb in front of the house next door.

She waited for me on the street, and it broke the ice when she took my hand. We walked the little way to her house.

Her house was neat as a pin. Her living room was bigger than mine, and her furniture was better than my apartment furniture. She gave me a quick tour of the three bedrooms, two bathrooms, small kitchen, dining room, and living room.

"Nice place," I said.

"I've lived here since I was five. It was my parents' house."

"So, who sleeps in the other bedrooms?"

"No one," she said.

"You feel safe here? I just mean, you live alone, and you got this fine body."

She laughed. I enjoyed Susie's laugh.

She walked into her kitchen and opened the little old refrigerator, white like the gas stove. The cabinetry was wood, and the floor was black and white ceramic tile. On the wall, knickknacks were hanging up. A black and white cat clock with a ticking tail, a sign that said, "Bless this house." Hooks with oven mitts. A little tin coffeepot was on the stove and a mug tree with four coffee mugs beside it. A strand of garlic and a couple of strands of chilis hung by the stove. My apartment kitchen was more modern, but this felt homey to me.

"I have beer," she said.

I could see it on the top shelf of her little refrigerator.

"I'm good."

We walked back into her living room, her loafers tapping on the hardwood floor.

"If I had known you might come over, I would have had

Canadian Club for you," Susie said, her eyes twinkling with a playful glint.

"It's okay. You know I don't drink and drive," I replied, giving her a reassuring smile.

"You want me to make you dinner?" she offered, her voice soft and inviting.

"No, I'm good. But you need to eat for sure."

"I'm good," she said, her lips curling into a gentle smile.

I moved closer, feeling the warmth radiate from her body. I put my arms around her waist, cupped that fine ass of hers, squeezed gently, and let go. The scent of her lavender perfume filled my senses.

"I'm going home," I said, reluctantly stepping back.

"Wait a sec, Jefe." It was her turn to put her arms around my waist, and she squeezed my butt, laughing. "Okay, you can go, Jefe," she said, kissing me on my chin, her lips soft and warm.

"You're a keg of dynamite, Susie."

I walked out of her house so hard that I was glad it was dark. I didn't look forward to being home alone but stopped at the Hat and took home a hamburger, double fries, and a chili tamale. I wondered what the morning meeting would be about.

I turned on the lights, leaving dinner on the kitchen table, and walked through my apartment. It was empty. I sat on the foot of my bed and pulled off my shoes, putting them into the closet. I went back into the living room, fed the fish, and turned on the turntable. It already had a stack of records on the autochanger. I went to the kitchen, took everything out of the bag, and put it on the dinette. I stared at it for a second. The music was playing, but the house was so empty. Just as I was going to dig in, I heard the front door open. I peeked out across the living room to see Elena closing the door behind her.

"Mike drove me," she said, double-timing toward me. I hugged her.

"Hungry? I bought enough for both of us," I said.

"Are you alone?"

"Of course. Why do you ask?"

She squeezed my butt through my jeans like she often did. I had a quick thought about Susie earlier.

We sat down at the table. I cut the hamburger and the tamale in half. We ate on the paper the food had been wrapped in. Hamburgers from The Hat are delicious but messy. She bit into hers. I saw a speck of yellow at the corner of her mouth.

"Wait. Don't move."

I leaned across the table and licked the mustard with my tongue. My pulse jumped when I touched her.

When we were done eating, we washed our faces at the kitchen sink, tossed the paper into the trash, and headed to the bedroom. Elena hit the living room lights. I turned off the turntable.

"No showers," she said. "I want it raw."

"You are getting nastier," I said.

"G, I didn't fuck Mike or even close. He was a perfect gentleman."

"I didn't think you had," I said. I don't know if it was true or not. I'd been trying not to think about it.

"Smell my pussy if you don't believe me."

I laughed.

"I'll smell your pussy because I love to, not to check for Mike's leavings."

"Gross!"

"Not grosser than your offer for me to smell you."

I do believe we were crazy about each other.

14

SAM THE MAN

I wanted to bring Elena with me to the breakfast meeting with Sam, but she wouldn't do it. She didn't know him, and he had invited me and not her. At six-twenty-five, I pulled into the deli parking lot on Brooklyn Avenue. Elena walked across the street to the all-night Mexican restaurant.

I was meeting Sam at an all-night deli.

When I walked in, a guy sitting in a booth waved at me. Sam was not a little guy. He was a lot older than me, but not old. He had on suit pants, older and more casual than my nice jeans. His well-worn suit coat was draped over a chair parked at our table and looked more comfortable than nice. He had a rugged look, two-or three-day's worth of beard, and a clean white t-shirt. A millionaire like he was said to be, why would he dress like that? Maybe to avoid intimidating me. We shook hands, and I sat across from him. A waitress appeared, an older lady. I noticed a long gray ponytail down her back. I ordered coffee, black.

"My order is in, George. The food here is good," Sam said.

I glanced at the breakfast menu. Looked like a hundred egg dishes. The only way I eat eggs is in an omelet.

"Denver Omelet," I told the waitress. "And a side of very crisp bacon, no toast."

"It's about time we meet," Sam said. "I've driven by the Brooklyn & Rowan shop, and every time the parking lot is full."

"You should have parked at Safeway and come in."

Sam laughed. "You should have valet parking," he countered. It was my turn to laugh.

"Come over, and I'll give you a tour of my facility," he said. "I have the entire block."

"I know. I go by there all the time," I lied, only about the all the time.

"When you have a free minute, drop by," he said. "I'd love to show you around."

"I will for sure," I said. "Be nice to see you at the main shop. I'm there all the time."

"You have a good reputation, George. You should be proud. Judge Black loves you."

"You know him?"

"For years. I don't see him much, but we talk on the phone."

I smiled. "I like Judge Black big time," I said.

My food arrived in about fifteen minutes. I was sure Sam was Jewish and wondered if they changed the rules about eating pork. Anyway, Sam knew his table manners. He waited for my food to arrive before he started on the full stack of pancakes and a side of ham.

"I like your mechanic, Jose," Sam said. "I don't know him that well at all, but he seems to be a good man."

I started on my Denver omelet. It was tasty.

"He's a good man," I said. "I'm lucky. My whole team is extraordinary. I've never fired anyone, and no one has quit."

Sam laughed. "It's too soon."

I shrugged. "Maybe so."

"Who finances your big equipment like the spray booth and oven?"

"My bank," I said. "My banker is very tight with personal loans, but he gives me whatever I need in equipment."

As soon as Sam put down his empty cup, the waitress refilled it, warmed up mine, and glided off. The booths and tables had filled up, and she was all over the place.

"I'm the owner of Eagle Finance. If you need a loan or want to buy equipment, the interest won't be as low as you pay the bank, but there's no fuss with me. Tell me what you need, and you got it."

"That's very kind of you," I said. "I'll keep that in mind."

"It's what I do," he said. "I have a suggestion. Give Jose another two stalls for mechanic work. I'll give you the best pricing like I'm doing now, and that's my payback for anything you need aside from auto parts."

"Jose has a helper now. He's busy."

"He told me he only has two stalls."

"He told you that?"

"George, I'm only saying that if you have room, expand the mechanic department. If you need any help, I'm a phone call away. Load of money to be made in mechanic work."

"I will check it out. I recently opened an upholstery department that is taking up some serious room."

"You make more money on mechanical," he said. "You know what else you should do?"

He wasn't grumpy like Matt, but something in him reminded me of him. He had lots of ideas about what I could do with the shop. I listened to them all.

When we got up to leave, we walked out together.

"I'm right here," he said as we came to a nice Cadillac Coupe Deville that needed a wash.

I put my hand out to shake his hand and got pulled into a bear-like hug.

"Give me a hug, son."

"It's been a pleasure, Sam."

"The other way around," he said. We shook hands, and he opened his car door.

I walked over to my Impala. Sam was gone before I got in. It was chilly, but I lowered the convertible top. I drove around the block and up to the restaurant where Elena was. Elena came out right away. Her lilting smile caught me by surprise and brightened my day.

"How did it go? Was it worth giving up our jog? G, aren't you cold?"

I left the top down, put the window up, and turned the heat on high.

The full pick-up truck in front of me took its time pulling out and turning left. We took a right.

"I think it was a good meeting. Sam is quite a character."

"I'm anxious to hear about your impression of him."

"You said you didn't know him."

"I know of him. At my high school, he gives a scholarship to someone in the graduating class. He's not from East Los Angeles either."

"He lives in West Los Angeles, Hancock Park. I don't know which one is his, but I've seen those mansions from the outside."

"What did he want to see you about?"

I described him to a T, including his eccentric appearance, and told her everything. When we got to the shop, I was still talking.

I raised the convertible top after I parked. Elena was laughing at me.

"Crazy man," she said. "Save it for summer."

"Can't wait," I said.

ELENA, Mike, and I were in my office at Eastland to discuss the new shop by the car wash. I had already been closed for an hour. There was a problem. The car wash had constant business. In Mike's words, "The place is packed all day long." But the car wash customers weren't jumping at the chance of painting their cars for thirty-five dollars.

Five cars a day didn't happen.

The first day open, Mike reported five paint jobs, two small body jobs. Two of those five jobs were on the house: the landlord and the car wash owner.

On the second day, two cars.

At the end of the week, it was clear that the shop would not break even.

Mike said, "But we only just opened."

"Sounds like my line to Elena about the Soto shop."

"Does sound familiar," Elena said.

"It would be nice to get to five a day," I said, "Plus, some bodywork."

"We're buried behind the car wash," Mike said. "The shop should be on the street side to get heavy traffic like on Brooklyn where you are."

I hadn't thought of that. I wish it had crossed my mind the day I jumped to lease the place. I do have my stupid moments.

"You already spent the money to set it up," Elena said. "All you have now is payroll and the basics."

"Payroll, basics, and next month we start paying rent," I said. "It's not just payroll. It's payroll taxes, insurance, and all the little things like supplies we bought to open and need to pay for within thirty days."

ON THE WAY HOME, Elena suggested we tighten up, again badmouthing the insurance work we were doing. I was driving. I felt her hand on my cheek. I took her hand and kissed it.

"I would be lost without you," I said.

"That's so sweet, G. Tell me that again."

I told her again.

Then she continued with business. "Eastland can take care of everything if the insurance drain stops."

"If I stop taking insurance work from the companies who send us business, I'll never get them back. And. I make a lot of money off insurance work."

Elena sighed. "Baby, stressing is not going to get more business at the car wash place. Baby, say it, it's okay."

"I love you," I heard myself say.

"That wasn't hard, was it?" Elena teased me.

I still had her hand near my mouth, and I nibbled it.

"You say it," I said.

"That's easy. I love you, George Hatcher."

Even back then, I had my emotional moments. I swallowed.

TWO WEEKS WENT BY. The shop by the car wash was nearly a total loss.

Elena and I were at the shop by the car wash. It was dead. Soldado, the bodyman, was playing solitaire with the masker. The painter was arguing with Mike about getting a homeless guy to walk around wearing a 'We Paint Cars for $35' sign out front. We were in the little office at the original desk that had been cleaned up, drinking coffee from a percolator that hadn't been paid for yet. The mugs we were using were from Eastland. Elena's arms were crossed on the desk, and she was resting her head in her arms, her eyes closed. "We should go back to Eastland and get some work done," she said.

"That meeting with Sam," I said. "Sam had all sorts of ideas on what I should do with what I already had. One of his ideas was that I should buy new cars that were sold as salvage to the junkyard, fix them up, and sell them."

"How does that work?" Elena's head popped up like a meerkat. She sat up.

"I'll call Sam right now for details."

Sam recommended a couple of junkyards where I could find newer salvaged cars. One of the places was a junkyard I was already doing business with when I needed used parts.

I had Alexa close up Eastland II to cover the floor with Susie at Brooklyn Avenue.

At the junkyard, I asked for Jeff and told him Sam had asked me to come over to scout out some cars. I had never been to the yard, and it was immense.

"It's like a vast rusty sea," Elena said, with her eyes wide, as we followed the signs to the office.

Instead of waves, there was row after row of cars, as far as the eye could see. In the center of it all was a small building where people worked and where employees and guests like us parked their cars.

"Sam called me and said to look out for you," Jeff said. "Let me show you around."

I knew there was some kind of organization, but I didn't see it. Jeff carried a clipboard with an indecipherable chart that may or may not have been a map.

For some of the cars, the word 'totaled' was totally appropriate.

He showed us a 1962 Mustang that was a total wreck from the back and another 1962 Mustang that had a perfect back but was smashed in the front.

"If you take these two, you cut, weld them together, redo the upholstery, paint the cars. It's less than a year old."

I pictured the possibilities right away.

Elena didn't say anything, but she was frowning.

"How much for both?"

"Five hundred, and I'll give you two pink slips. When you're done, use the pink slip with the serial number of the front chassis."

"I'll give you four hundred," I said. "If it works, I'll be back and buy all the time."

"If I charge you four hundred, I need to charge you a hundred to drop them off at your shop."

I took five hundred in cash out of my pocket and paid him on the spot. Elena watched in disbelief.

"Just like that? No 'Let me think about it,' or something sane?"

I laughed, and then Jeff did too.

I gave them the address of the new shop.

Elena and I drove to the new shop. Soldado was sitting on a bench. No work. The masker was masking one car. The painter was helping her.

Mike, Elena, and I went into the office. I told Mike what we were trying out until there was more business.

"I need to see the cars," Mike said.

"They will both be here in two hours."

Soldado to me in Spanish, "I never did it before, but I can use a torch really good, and with an electric welder, I'm even better."

I remember when I was welding on rooftops doing rough air conditioning jobs with Matt. I can hold my own in welding.

Mike walked us to an area of the shop with some boxes up against the wall. No particular department had been assigned there yet.

"Let's put it over here in the corner so it doesn't interfere with whatever business we do get."

"No sweat. Put it where you want. I'll be back tomorrow, and we can figure out what we're going to do when the cars are here."

"How do you plan to sell the car?"

"I'll worry about that when we have a car to sell."

Mike gave me a playful salute. I think he had mixed feelings. I knew he was worried about the shop's success and wanted to manage it himself, but he was optimistic that this new project would bring in money and maybe turn things around.

Elena and I exited, laughing all the way to the car.

"Do you think Soldado is good enough at bodywork to put that Mustang together?"

"He's been doing it for seven years. I hope so." I had confidence in him.

"I hope so, too," Elena said.

When Elena and I returned the next afternoon, the cars were there. Soldado was already pulling out the seats of the car with the perfect back end. He had stripped the carpet, exposing the metal floor.

I saw a box of nuts and bolts.

"Packrat much?" I asked.

He didn't take offense. He explained that he was organizing a shop box for nuts, bolts, and small pieces that he would need for reassembly and future jobs.

"In couple hours, this car will look like one of those Chinese taxis," Soldado said in Spanish.

I laughed. "You mean a rickshaw," I said in English.

Mike laughed. "He's right. Without the smashed front end, it will be like a rickshaw." He looked at the smashed-up parts. "What do we do with leftovers?"

Soldado said, "We can use some of this." He took the lug nuts out of a flat tire and put them in his box.

"All of it?" Mike asked.

"Not all of it," Soldado said. "There's your junk," pointing out a crushed fender, a ton of identifiable parts, more metal that was no longer identifiable, a pile of rubber from the former tire company, carpet pieces, and who knows what else.

I was glad to see he wasn't the car hoarder Ramirez had been.

"Call the junkyard, make a deal for them to come get it. Next time, I'll be sure to include it when I buy the next salvage."

"You plan to do this more than once?" Mike asked.

"If it pays off, sure."

Sam had told me, "Keep a man rebuilding salvage cars, and you'll make money on it every time." And Sam was a man who knew how to make money.

I picked up a cutting torch. The acetylene and oxygen tanks were on a dolly with a chain across the front. I wanted to light up the torch so bad, but I didn't.

"I got good with one of these."

"Is that what he'll use to cut away the front of the car?" Elena asked.

I looked at Soldado. "This is it," I said. "Right?"

"Yes, Jefe," Soldado said. "When I weld the two halves together, I will use electric."

I nodded.

We didn't come back until Mike said he had a whole Mustang for us to see.

Elena and I drove to the car wash shop, which was surprisingly quiet. Only two cars were being serviced, excluding the Mustang, and the waiting room was empty, with no phones ringing. It had been thirteen days since our last visit, and the car looked pristine, almost like a new used car. The Mustang sported that eye-catching orange hue typical of its model. I opened the doors to inspect the weld on the rocker panels beneath the door. To my satisfaction, there was no visible seam where the two sections were joined; Soldado had done an excellent job. With no carpet in place yet, it was easy to see that Soldado had welded with near perfection, then expertly ground it down without compromising the integrity of the weld. The seats were back in, leaving the finishing touches to my trimmer, Paulo, and his brother to match everything seamlessly.

I drove the car back to the main shop with Elena behind me. The car drove fine. It had a good motor but pulled right when I used the brakes. I parked on Olympic Boulevard, got out of the car, and Elena parked behind me.

"What's wrong?"

"Let's drop it off at an alignment shop down the street here on Olympic. It's pulling to the right."

"Can't Jose do it?"

"We don't have the alignment equipment."

As I drove the rebuilt Mustang, I hoped it wasn't too serious. I think that Soldado would have caught that when the cars were bare bones.

The alignment shop was on the property of Haru's Automatic Transmission. I had not been there before, but I knew the big corner.

I met the owner, Haru Tatsui. He was older than Elena and me, but not by much. He had a genuine smile going all the time we were there. He looked over the car, then back at Elena. He could not keep his eyes off Elena, even when he was talking to me.

"I took two cars, cut them in half, and this is what I got. It's pulling to the right," I said.

Haru gave the car and me a double-take before returning to Elena.

"You did what?"

THE NEXT DAY, Haru and another guy delivered the Mustang.

"It aligned with no problem. Frame is good."

"Hey, I appreciate you bringing it over."

"No problem. I want to see your place."

I handed the invoice he gave me to Elena. I gave him a tour while Elena wrote a check. We were packed. The magic cash cow.

When he left, I said to Elena, "He came over just to get another look at you."

"His eyes bored holes in me yesterday."

"Oh, you noticed."

She stuck her tongue out at me. "Of course, I noticed."

I shot a kiss at her.

I MADE a deal with Paulo to take the interior back to the original cream color of the front-end interior instead of the back-half's fire-engine red.

The upholstery department was keeping busy. About half of Paulo's work was from car dealers on Atlantic Boulevard, the same car dealers I had passed out brochures to.

As it turned out, I didn't need their paint business. I was at capacity. Paulo was smart and knew how to deal with the car people. He was busy and kept his brother busy too. I got money from him, but it came in dribbles. I hadn't figured out if I was making money on the department or not, but it did draw customers.

"You are making some money, but I think Paulo is not accounting for all the work he is doing," Elena said.

"When he's solid on his feet, I'm going to get out of the partner business and have him pay rent. That way, no paperwork or being suspicious of him."

"G, good idea."

I HAD PLANNED to park the Mustang outside the car wash shop with a for sale sign. I have a vivid memory of parking this first reconstructed car on the Safeway parking lot with a sign, fifteen hundred dollars, fourteen hundred miles, with my business card stapled on the sign. I sent Jose to take a drive with the interested customer. Right after the ride, the man went home and came back with the green cash. Before we closed the shop that day, the car was sold.

I called Sam, who was still working.

"I wanted to give you a customer to finance the first car," I told Sam, "but he came up with cash."

"Kid, if you were here, I'd give you a big hug."

THAT NIGHT, we celebrated at home. I don't remember what dinner was. Leftovers? Hot dogs? Salad?

We had a couple of drinks of CC water. We liked to drink it, no question. We didn't drink it every day, though.

At home in the kitchen, with the CC water on the table, we figured out what we made on the car.

"So, tell me what the expenses were," Elena said, pencil in hand. She scribbled down the numbers and added them up.

We added up the cost of rebuilding the car, which I had estimated on my own before I priced it at fifteen hundred. The expenses: five hundred plus fifty to send back the leftover parts, labor, and materials for bodywork, the paint job, Paulo's upholstery, Jose's tune-up, and matching new tires. We had a thousand dollars in the car.

"You're in the black," Elena said, "That's okay."

We moved into the living room. I sat on the upholstered chair in front of the television that was on.

"I don't think I priced it right."

"Baby, you sold it in a couple of hours. Give me a break, please. It practically sold itself."

"Let's find another one tomorrow. This time I'm not going to say yes so fast."

The six o'clock news was over. Some Western was playing: Bonanza, Wagon Train, Rawhide, The Virginian, one of those. Elena walked over to the TV and turned off the sound-in a couple of hours when the movie was scheduled, we'd turn the sound on. Elena moved to sit on my lap.

"Sorry about dinner," she said. "We can have lunch tomorrow somewhere nice."

"You got it," I said, my arms around her.

15

RESTORING JUNKED CARS

If your twenties are miles away in your rearview mirror, maybe you've forgotten how it was - we did it whenever we wanted, and in the morning, we did it when we woke up. With Elena and me, our thing was always about business and sex. It just was. As we jogged, the Mustang was on our minds. "Clearing five hundred dollars is like ten cars with paint and bodywork," I said. Elena looked at me with that spark in her eye and said, "I could fuck you for that." Yeah, that's how we rolled.

WE DID NOT GO STRAIGHT to the junkyard but spent a couple of hours at Eastland, planning to go to lunch after finding the next project car. Jeff had a car ready and waiting for us, a year-old two-door Buick with a smashed rear end. I couldn't figure out why insurance would have totaled it. Jeff was grinning like a prospector who panned a gold nugget.

"It has less than a thousand miles," Jeff said.

"Why did they total it?"

"My guess is the owner thought he'd never have a new car again. Some carriers are good people."

"How much?"

"Eight hundred," Jeff said.

"Jeff, I have to buy new parts for this. I can't do eight."

"Seven fifty, and I deliver it."

I looked at Elena. She returned a blank expression like we were playing poker and turned to face my Impala as if all that was on her mind was lunch.

"I can do six," I said. "I have that much in cash." I walked around the car and stopped to scowl at the damage on the rear end like it was the worst thing on the planet.

"Six fifty," Jeff countered.

"I'll think about it," I said, looking at my watch. "We're both hungry. Going to have lunch." I took one step toward the Impala.

"George, wait. Give me the six."

"You got a pink slip?"

"George, give me a break. Of course, I got a pink."

Once in my car, Elena revealed her excitement. "The interior is perfect," she said.

"I know, I saw, but I didn't want to let on I liked it too much."

"Baby, you rock."

She leaned over the console and planted a kiss on my lips.

SOLDADO TURNED that car around in a week, but he had to wait a week for parts from Buick. It was just under two weeks until I parked it at Safeway. This time, the sign said, "Eighteen hundred dollars, eight hundred fifty-five miles. Come across the street." My business card was again stapled on the sign.

The buyer wanted to negotiate, but I didn't budge. The buyer wanted to finance a thousand. I sent him to Eagle Finance.

Sam called me in the morning. "I just gave the buyer a check payable to you for a thousand, and he has eight hundred in cash. Send me the pink slip."

"I'll bring it over myself," I said and did.

"Maybe we should buy two cars, if he has them," I told Elena.

"Baby, where you going to put the second car?" she asked.

When we went to the salvage yard, Jeff offered us soft drinks.

I bought a black and white Mercury Meteor with rear damage and two thousand miles on it for three hundred and fifty dollars. I figured new parts would make it like new. I also got a Chevy station wagon with smashed front bumpers and fenders. I didn't think it had frame damage.

"Put one outside where it is not a distraction," I told Mike on the phone.

The shop's weekly average was two or three a day, so Soldado had time to do the restoration work. I gave him a bonus for the Mustang, and for each car he worked on.

That was the beginning of my salvage restoration business.

At the time, California did not require a pink slip to state that the car was salvaged, so people didn't ask that question. The guy who bought the Mustang came back to get some custom upholstery work. He loved the car. I don't know what he would have said if I had shown him the two cars cut in half before they were welded together. One thing for certain: if he found out and came to me to complain, I would buy the car back. No argument.

I CUT BACK on how much work my accountant did for me. He still did the important stuff, but I no longer let him write the checks. If I needed help filing paid or pending bills, Elena was there to do the work. We were together all the time anyway. I was going to handle the paychecks but stopped it after the first time I calculated deductions. I let Donald punch those numbers. "I need you were the first words when I called. Help."

Donald came over. He treated me like I was his only client and I knew that was not the case.

"I'll be glad to do it for you," Donald said. "And you can walk over and pick up the checks. I don't need to do it here."

I never slacked off writing checks for the suppliers. As Donald had done for so long, I fudged payroll taxes and sales tax due to the State Board of Equalization. By holding back, I didn't run as short at the end of the month and didn't have to hit Chester for double digits. I was fooling myself. All I was doing was building debt to California and the IRS, who charged immense penalties and interest. I didn't know that before because I always paid them timely.

So, I got mail from the IRS and the state to pay up. I put the notices in my desk drawer, figuring a trip to Vegas might make enough to clear it all off.

Time passed, and I wasn't paying attention.

Elena was helping me with the Monday deposit.

"There's never any mess in your desk. I've never seen anything so organized," Elena said. "So why do you have a drawer full of payroll and sales tax reports that I don't think you paid."

She had cleared off the top of the desk and emptied out the drawer. The deposit cash she was handling was in a stack on the desk. Beside my brand-new IBM Selectric typewriter, there was the wooden divider with everything from interchangeable type balls in different fonts, ink, re-inkable ribbons to white out to rubber bands. A stack of quarters and a roll of dimes were in a little bowl. The payroll papers were in a neat stack. The sales tax reports were in another stack right beside them. Alarm bells should have gone off in my head.

"I shouldn't have stopped Donald writing checks," I said. "He wrote the checks. I mailed them. I had to hustle to cover what was mailed. I mailed the reports but not the checks."

"Oh baby, you haven't paid it?" Elena's face fell.

"Nope."

"Fuck-Me," she said.

"Okay. Here and now?" I started unbuckling my belt.

"I didn't mean fuck me now," she said.

"Ouch," I said, leaving the belt on.

"If you were a kid, I'd spank you."

She put everything back in the desk except for the cash for the deposit tomorrow.

"Baby, you're the one that likes spankings," I said. She didn't laugh.

She threw the pen at me, nailed me in the chest.

"Ouch," I said again.

"That explains why you haven't run as short," she said gloomily. "I'd hoped it was the car sales."

"Exactly," I said. "I should have followed Ramirez's advice. No payroll. Pay cash. No sales tax. I'd be in the clear right now."

"You always managed to cover everything, meeting the problem head on, not hiding it in a drawer."

She stirred something defensive inside of me.

"Hiding from who? That's my desk. That's my drawer. Not hiding anything."

She got up and walked out of my office.

I moved to my chair and finished the deposit, sealed it in an envelope, and put it in the safe.

I'm sure that was the first time that Elena and I had an

exchange like that. Not an argument but close. I was pissed at myself for the hiding thing. I made such a big deal out of it. With Elena, such shenanigans were unnecessary. I kept no secrets from her.

When I went down to the shop floor, most of the lights were out, the gates were closed. Elena and Susie had closed up. Standing near the entrance, they were both smoking cigarettes.

Susie smoked but not inside the shop. When Elena first came to work, she smoked all the time, especially when she worked in the office upstairs. She didn't smoke much anymore.

"Are we ready?" I asked.

"I'm going to walk to my aunt's," Elena said. "She said I got a phone call today and one yesterday at the house. No message. I'll spend the night, see if I can catch the call, and find out why someone would call me there."

"I can drop you off there while you go in," I said.

"It's okay, G." She kissed me lightly on the lips and walked through the gates.

Susie was still around when I closed and padlocked the gates.

"You need a ride?" I asked, wondering why she hadn't crossed the street to the streetcar stop.

The cigarette was gone, but I could still smell it.

"Elena said you don't like to be alone, and I should go with you. But not if you don't want."

"She told you that?" A stupid question. "If you stay over, you know you need to jog with me in the morning."

"Cool," she said. "I'll have to borrow shorts from Elena's stuff."

A moment later, we were in the car.

"Hungry?"

She nodded.

I drove to Shakey's Pizza and wondered if I'd see Olivia.

16

NO MAGIC IN BEING ALONE

Susie kept the conversation going as I drove, so I didn't have room in my brain to wonder why Elena would just head to her aunt's house. I should have wondered if her visit to her aunt's was over my not paying my taxes or telling her that the desk and drawer were mine and I wasn't hiding anything.

Shakey's was lively and noisy. I had known that it would be that way, and I welcomed the raucous, friendly atmosphere that surrounded us. Susie and I sat shoulder-to-shoulder, somehow isolated by the noise around us. We talked as if we weren't in a room packed with noise, music, pizza, and strangers. I talked.

"Was Elena angry or upset when she came down from the office?"

"I didn't notice anything different except she asked me for a cigarette. Why do you ask? Did you have a fight?"

"I don't think so," I said.

It took me fifty years to realize what a lame answer that was.

I asked the waitress about Olivia. She didn't know Olivia was working that shift, so I guessed that she had moved on. It was strange, but I didn't even know her last name.

I ordered two beers and a pizza. We couldn't finish it, so the pizza came home with us in a box. At the house, I fixed us a couple of CC waters. We clicked glasses, had a toast, walked into the bedroom, set the glasses down, and went right to bed.

Susie rolled to her stomach and raised her fine ass. I pushed deep inside her.

"I can't believe I have you all to myself," she said.

"I'm thinking the same."

The few times the three of us had been in bed together, it had been almost like this. It's not like I can fuck both of them at the same time.

In that position, I couldn't see Susie's face, so I fantasized that it was Emma. Then I became rattled with myself. Why think of anyone else when Susie was a full package, in and out.

"Susie, get on top. I want to look at your beautiful face. You're an absolute turn-on."

She blushed. "Am I really beautiful?"

I kissed her. "You better believe it."

I still feel her lips on mine right now, decades later.

"Can we stay awake all night?" She said this at the height of the sex that was taking place at that moment.

I didn't reply. I pressed my lips harder against hers.

I SKIPPED THE JOG. While I was in the shower and before she got in the shower, Susie made coffee. I've never figured out how the smell of coffee can permeate the air like it does, but I came out, and the coffee fragrance greeted me.

"Jefe. Can you take me to my house so I can change clothes? I promise it will be fast. "

"Baby, don't call me Jefe." I smiled.

"You're my boss. You never said anything before."

"Okay. It's just that after last night it makes me feel bad that you are calling me boss."

She kissed me. "How about G then?"

"That works better," I said.

I kept wondering if Elena would be back that morning. If she did show, what would she say? Had we had a fight? What would I say? Ask her why she told Susie to go home with me.

I stripped the bed and stuffed the linens in the overloaded laundry bag. On the way to the shop, I dropped it off at the cleaners for fluff, dry, and fold. I hadn't taken the time to make the bed with the spare sheets. Susie wisely didn't say anything about the laundry. I drove by her house. She ran in barefoot, carrying her shoes. I sat in the car for three minutes, the fastest, quickest change of any woman I'd ever known. She came out the same way, in fresh clothes but barefoot and carrying her shoes that she put on in the car.

"Thanks, Jefe," she said. "Was that fast enough?"

TEN MINUTES BEFORE OPENING TIME, I pulled into my parking spot. Both entrances were already open. Elena was attending an early customer. She glanced up as Susie, and I neared the entrance. We all said good morning.

I left Susie working the floor with Elena, and I walked up to my office. I pulled out the copies of the reports I had mailed without checks. I went through all the reports and wrote down what I owed on each one. As I was finishing up, Elena walked in with two cups of coffee.

"You read my mind," I said. "Thank you."

She sat where I had been sitting when she threw the pen at me.

"Whatcha doing?"

I looked at her and reached for my coffee.

"Figuring out how much I owe for taxes."

"That's a good start."

It was awkward. We hadn't kissed. That never happened.

"I'm sorry I made a big deal out of the desk last night. You were right. How could you be hiding anything in your own desk?" She sipped her hot coffee.

"Are we good?" I asked.

Her smile was like a beam of light, like spring rain on a parched desert, like the brightness of cotton candy melting into sweetness. "We're good."

"Can we seal it with a kiss?"

She walked around my desk. I swiveled left in time for her to sit on my lap.

Our lips locked.

I'm not sure if it was my sigh or her sigh that I heard. Then the intercom on the phone went on.

"Help," Susie said. "Customers lined up."

We kissed again and looked out through the louvers. We saw two customers in line, and one more car was pulling in the lot. Elena started for the door.

"I'll be down as soon as I add all this up."

"We can handle it," she said and was gone.

I OWED twenty-one thousand in sales tax to the state, plus only they knew how much in penalties and interest. I owed thirty-four thousand to the IRS for the deductions I had withheld from the employees and the Eastland employer contribution. It was so stupid that I had everyone, even the couple that cleaned up, on the payroll.

I told myself I would figure a way to pay the taxes. Other than that, I was kind of stable until the end of the month. I had over seventy thousand dollars in insurance receivables. Even if I got paid all the money that day, after paying the past due taxes, it would not leave me much. Something was wrong. Where was my profit? How could things get worse? I remembered all the money I had won in Vegas. Where did it vanish to?

Holmberg called from the bank.

"George, the IRS served us a levy against Eastland's account."

"I'm sorry," I said. "How much is it?"

"The levy is twelve-thousand five hundred and change. Actually, you have enough in the account."

"I owe them more than that. This is only part of it."

"A day at a time," he said in that patient voice of his.

"I have checks out against all the money in that account. The only reason I have a balance is that the checks haven't hit the bank yet."

"Keep making daily deposits. I'll pay your checks when you don't have enough to cover it. When I do that, everyone sees the overdraft. You need to cover right away."

"I appreciate this," I said. "I have a deposit later today."

I had never been overdrawn at the bank. Checks were not mailed out until I had the checks covered, which is where Chester came in. If I didn't have enough, I floated a check with Chester, deposited the money in the bank, and the checks were covered. The only person I had to pay back was Chester. That moment, I didn't have a float with Chester, but it wasn't the end of the month yet.

At noon Elena picked up our lunch from the meat market. I ordered an all-steak burrito with guacamole and nothing else in it. When we were done, Susie would go to lunch at one. We sat on the leather sofa where we always ate, the food between us. We turned to face each other. I kept saying that one day I would buy a small table with at least two chairs.

"Tell me about last night with Susie," Elena said, picking up her taquito.

"Come on, you already know."

"G, you are a sex freak," she bit at her taquito. "I can say that because I'm one, too."

"It wasn't even about sex. You left me in a daze," I said. "You just took off to your aunt's house."

The way she held the taquito, the way she looked at me when she bit into it, the way she licked the trace of guacamole from her fingertip. She was sexy even when she ate.

"I fixed you up, didn't I?" Her eyes laughed over the top of the taquito.

"Baby, thanks for that, but you know I have no problem fixing myself up."

"Temper," she teased. She swiped it into a bowl of guac and held the taquito up to my mouth. I took a bite. I did the same with my burrito and held it there until she swallowed what she had in her mouth then took a bite.

"Delicious," she said. "The cook loves you."

"It's you he loves."

Elena laughed.

We ate silently for maybe a minute, but I was too curious to keep quiet.

"You said you were getting calls at your aunt's. Did you solve the mystery?"

"Remember the Texan in Hawaii, where I stayed for six months? When he gave me the five thousand, I gave him that number when I left."

"What does he want?"

"He wants me to go back to Hawaii. I told him no."

"Why?"

She gave me a don't-you-know look, swallowed her food, and said, "He likes young Vajayjay. My vajayjay. There's no love between us. Never was."

"Why did you tell him no?"

"I had enough of Hawaii. I'm too young to retire and lay in the sun. It's great, but after a while, I would be drinking like crazy to keep from dying of boredom."

"I'm sure he'll try again."

She nodded and crumpled her napkin. "He has other houses in the US. He owns a piece of a casino in Vegas. He's into everything."

We finished eating and tossed the paper plates, cups, and bags into the little trash bin by the desk. The food was gone, but the scent of chili, garlic, cheese, and cumin remained. I could also smell the unfinished cup of coffee on my desk, and the faint scent of Elena's perfume that reminded me of lime and chilis and something else I could not put my finger on.

It wasn't quiet. Downstairs, the sound of street traffic was the background noise. Someone had the radio on. People were talking, the voices indistinct. The compressor cut in and out. Someone was sanding, someone was painting, Jose was running power tools. I loved the sound of the shop in action.

She stood and faced me, put her arms around my neck.

"Baby. Don't be jealous of the Texan. He's like Susie. Neither are threats to you and me. Did I say that right?"

"I didn't have to fuck Susie."

"It's okay that you did it. She's so sweet."

We kissed.

"Wait," she said. "You owe me."

When she flipped the office louvers closed, it was almost like the acoustic ceiling tiles kicked in. It was not silent by any means, but the sound from below was much muted. It was like we were in our own little bubble of privacy.

Elena walked over to the sofa and focused her eyes on mine. Her shoes and jeans came off. She lay back on the sofa and raised her arms, beckoning me. The faint scent of her reminded me of my naïve encounter with Valita when I was about ten years old.

We didn't relieve Susie for lunch until thirty minutes past one.

When we finally went downstairs, Susie gave Elena a knowing smile and kiss.

ON THE NOISY SHOP FLOOR, Elena and I had no customers to wait on. We got busy with paperwork against a wall of white noise. The spray booth exhaust fan was whirling away over a robin's egg blue Chevy Malibu. The heat lamps of the car oven hummed to the black Chrysler Imperial inside it. When it was dry, the Chevy would take its place. A Ferraro GTO was quietly getting masked for fire engine red and a pinstripe, expensive because of new matching red upholstery, the pinstripe, and one of Jose's famous tune-ups. Jose, the mechanic, was making a lot of noise with his power tools. He now had four stalls, and they were occupied, which made Sam happy. Of Sam's several businesses, his primary was the auto parts he sold directly to mechanics. His company rebuilt almost everything under the hood of a car, including motors.

ELENA and I gave Susie a ride that night, pulling over to the curb in front of her house. After she was safely inside, I pulled back onto the street and headed for home. It was night, and as we drove, the streetlights briefly illuminated inside the car. I glanced to my right and caught Elena watching me.

After we dropped her off, Elena asked, "How did you know where she lived?"

"I dropped her off one night," I said. "She was going to make me dinner. I went inside but left ten minutes later."

I got caught by a red light. It was dark in the car. I felt Elena's fingertips on my face.

"I love you all the more because you don't lie."

I didn't say anything. The light changed, and I moved forward in the flow of traffic. She moved her hand from my face, took my right hand from the steering wheel, and put my index finger in her mouth, then my middle finger.

These are moments I can't forget.

17

MY NEIGHBORS' PIMP

I had spent years jogging. Elena was still new to it, but she could jog and talk. I had trouble doing that, but it didn't stop me from talking. We were running shoulder-to-shoulder one corner away from that big hill that had once defeated her. It didn't defeat her anymore.

It was cooler in the morning. Sometimes there was fog that turned everything into a foreign landscape. This was one of those foggy mornings. You could taste the city on your tongue. So, there we were, only the sounds of our labored breathing, our tennis-shoed feet in the early morning, cars making their way past us out of the neighborhood, the occasional horn or screech.

"You need to pay the taxes before they attach your account again," Elena said, not gasping at all.

"Believe me, I'm not ignoring it." Pause, "Holmberg said he'll cover me," Pause, "...when I don't have enough money for checks that come in," Pause, "...but when the bank gets a writ of attachment," Pause, "...everyone knows about it. Even if he's the manager," Pause. "...if he extends the courtesy of paying my checks," Pause, "...when I don't have the money," Pause, "...it's going to kick him in the ass." My sentences came across as gulps of air with a pause between them.

"How do you know that?"

"He explained it," Pause, "As bank manager, he's got limited leverage," Pause, "Holmberg can lend me fifty thousand to buy equipment," Pause, "... use the equipment I buy as collateral, no problem," Pause, "If I want a line of credit, I'm only good for about seventy-five hundred. That's..." Pause, "...nothing."

"I love you, George Hatcher."

We reached the very steep street to the top of Monterey Hills, where the great big homes were. Talk was done. Not even Elena could talk and jog that one.

WE SPLIT up at the apartment, showered alone, dressed, and had coffee and pan dulce she had brought home from the meat market.

"Too good," I said.

"We earned it after the jog."

"Damn straight, we did."

We were doing dishes, minutes from leaving for work, when I heard a rapid knock at the door and the doorbell. Elena and I heard it at the same time and looked at each other. I was washing, Elena, drying.

"A visitor this early?" Elena said.

By the time I reached the door, the bell had gone off again, and knocking was urgent.

I opened the door with Elena behind me, drying her hands on the dishtowel.

It was Emma.

"George, so sorry to intrude, but fucking Jaimie is beating up Ava. Help us, please."

I ran behind Emma to their apartment on the other side of the pool. No one was out. It was not even seven yet. The fog from earlier had cleared.

Emma opened the door, and I charged through it. I could see Ava on the carpet floor, her arms curled protectively across her face and head. Jaime was standing over her with his back to me, his hands in fists. He couldn't see me come in. He and Emma were yelling, so I doubt he heard me.

"Stop!" Emma was yelling, not just that. She was yelling whole sentences trying to get him to stop, and Ava was sobbing on the floor. I had no idea what the words were. I saw red.

I grabbed him by the back of his head. His long ponytail was a convenient handle. I jerked him back so hard that a good handful of hair came out of my hand. I dropped it to the floor as he screamed. He turned around, and I belted him in about the same place I had hit him with the fire extinguisher.

"I'll call the police," Elena said.

I hadn't noticed that she followed us.

Emma caught Elena's arm and said, "No police. We can't have police."

"What are you? Their fucking bodyguard or something?"

I punched him a second time, my fist twisting, going for his midsection, deep in his belly. He was soft, and my fist was still making contact when he went down.

"Prick!"

The word prick came out of him with the blast of air from my punch. I didn't say anything, but that punch hurt my right hand. Jamie went down. Elena and Emma pulled Ava to her feet. As soon as she was up, Ava kicked him in the ribs with her tennis shoes. Emma was barefoot and stomped him many times in succession, hammering his stomach. He groaned and then yelled in rage.

I went down on my knees and got right up to his red face. I grabbed his collar and held him up by my right hand.

"Remember what I told you before?" I yanked him up and dropped him back to the floor. I heard him wheeze. "I told you I was going to send some very nasty people after you if you ever touched Ava or Emma again. Time to start sleeping with one eye open, motherfucker, because that message is going out today. There won't be any place safe for you."

Jaime got to his knees, glaring at me, wild-eyed in his red-faced rage. He lunged.

I hit him again.

"This is just a preview," I said.

Elena touched my arm lightly. "George, enough."

I turned to face Elena.

"Are you okay?" I asked Ava, who had sunk down into a chair.

Jaimie managed to get to his feet, staggered out the door, and was gone.

"My stomach. The bastard punched me four times. He doesn't want to mess up my face because it messes up business."

It was a good thing he was gone by the time I heard that.

Emma said, "I'll take care of her. George, thank you." She patted Elena's shoulder. "Your name is Elena, right?"

Elena nodded.

"Sorry, Elena," Emma said.

Elena hugged Emma. "It's okay."

We both hugged Ava.

"If you must have a pimp, get a new one," I said. "This bastard is a sick fuck."

Elena and I walked to my apartment. I took off my bloody T-shirt and put on a clean one from the laundry. Elena put the shirt in the bathroom sink in cold water. I hadn't said anything about my hand, but I guess I favored it enough for Elena to notice. Elena took a look at my hand. It was swollen, but that was nothing to the damage I did to Jaimie.

"Is your hand going to be okay? We're out of ice."

She gave me a wet dishtowel, one piece of ice in it. I wrapped it around my hand.

"I can ice it at the shop if I have to," I said. "Maybe you should drive."

We walked down the back stairs to my car in the parking garage. Elena opened the car door for me. It can be surprisingly difficult to do one-handed.

Elena pulled us into traffic. Her eyes were on the road.

"I knew you could fight, but today, you seemed in a rage."

"I don't like men who hit women," I said. "I hate it."

"Do you hate it because you witnessed it in your life?"

"No, I never witnessed it."

"I've never been hit by any man," she said. "I'd find a way to kill him."

"I'd kill him for you."

"Are you really going to send someone over to his house?"

I thought of Pi and how easy that would be.

"I'll know when I cool off. This is not the first time he's done this."

"If it happened before and the girls didn't learn from it, what else can you do? Keep protecting them? It's not your fight."

"I don't have the answer. I prefer working on a way to pay my taxes."

Elena smiled, her eyes straight ahead. We were driving along Floral to Brooklyn Avenue.

"Now you're talking, Champ."

I chuckled. "Champ?"

"Yeah, your new handle."

"I could fuck you right this minute," I said, ignoring the pain from my hand.

She braked, pulled to the curb, and stopped with a big smile on her face and eyes wide open.

"Yeah?" she said, "I'll take you up on that right here, right now. I'll sit on you right where you are."

I chickened out.

"Drive, baby," I said, laughing.

18

I KEPT LEARNING

It was Wednesday morning. The ten cars scheduled for the day were written up and processed through the system. Those needing bodywork would receive it first. The cars that only required paint were water-sanded, and then all the windows and chrome were papered and taped up for the spray booth. About two out of ten cars were paint jobs that cost more than the popular $35. The preparation for these cars was the same; the only difference was the paint and colors, which weren't available at the lower price.

A marshal's car pulled up, and a uniformed man came out of his car. A man in civilian clothes got out of the passenger side. When he started walking towards the entrance, I noticed he had an overnight bag, a briefcase, and a bedroll.

I had thought it was another judge, but the civilian with a bedroll was no judge. Something was up, and I had no clue what it was. Neither did Elena.

Elena pointed to his car and asked the marshal, "Are you here to get that painted?"

The marshal said, "Not today. I'm looking for George Hatcher, president of Eastland Auto Center."

"That's me," I said, stepping in his direction.

Everyone in the shop had stopped working. They were all looking in our direction like a bunch of nosy meerkats.

"Back to work, people," Elena said. "This ain't no sideshow."

"Yes, ma'am," Jose said. He, Luis, and their assistants went back into their areas, but I figured they were listening because it was much quieter than usual. At least there wasn't a line of customers watching.

As we walked toward the customer's waiting area, I heard Susie say to somebody really loud, "Why are you sitting on your ass? That car's not going to fix itself!"

Then it got noisy again.

The marshal handed me a stack of legal pages stapled together.

"I'm here on a writ of execution from the State Board of Equalization to install Mr. Keller here as a keeper until the sum of eighteen-thousand seven-hundred and ten dollars is paid. None of this is necessary if you have eighteen thousand seven hundred ten dollars in cash to satisfy this writ. Do you have the money?"

I shook my head. "I don't have that much money, no."

"In that case, the keeper, Mr. Keller, stays."

"Officer, mind explaining what all this means? I'm a total novice at this," I said.

The civilian stepped up.

"I'm Jim Keller, the keeper. I move in here today, and I will stay here twenty-four hours a day, seven days a week, collecting all money paid to your business until the sum the marshal mentioned is paid in full. I add a hundred-fifty dollars a day to that amount for every day I'm here. The state adds penalties and interest every day as well."

"How do you do that?"

"Put me somewhere so you are not embarrassed by the customers. When something is paid, I take it all. At the end of the day, I give you a receipt for all the money I received."

"Elena, pinch me so I can wake up." I was only half-kidding.

Elena pinched my right upper arm.

The marshal and the keeper did not laugh.

I didn't make a fuss.

"Elena, take him up to the office to see if he's okay with being up there, and I'll walk over to see my attorney to explain how this works."

Keller chuckled at my comment. The marshal walked to his car and drove off.

Carlos Navarro was only two blocks away, about the same distance as my accountant Donald. I walked fast, seriously wondering if I was going to wake up at any moment. It did not feel real. I made it to Carlos's office, and his receptionist let me straight in.

Carlos was in his office, signing a stack of papers. Luckily, he had no other clients with him. As soon as I said the words 'keeper' and 'marshal,' he caught on.

"Son, never, never, not pay the State of California and the IRS. The state is petty. They bring in a guy to stay day and night. He takes the keys, and no assets go anywhere except to him. Everything that comes in, he takes it."

"That's exactly what he told me."

"Did you bring the papers he served you with?"

"Damn, I should have."

"Let's walk to the shop. I'll try and call the state board and try to make a deal. Do you have any part of the money?"

"I can cash a check for about eight thousand. It will be a floater. I don't think I have enough to cover it."

Carlos looked confused. "A floater?"

"Never mind. I can get eight thousand, for sure."

"The keeper is not going to take a check from you."

"I'll go to the gas station and get the cash. I can't get more than that without giving him some notice."

"How about the balance?"

"Carlos, the keeper says he is there for eighteen thousand. I owe more than that. It just hasn't gotten to collections yet, or he'd know about it."

I WENT UP to my office with Carlos and left him with the keeper. An hour went by.

Carlos talked to the keeper's supervisor and worked out an agreement. The agreement was that I would give the keeper ten thousand in cash, and the balance would be paid to a State Board of Equalization Office in two weeks at the latest. Chester gave me the ten thousand in return for four checks, each in the amount of twenty-five hundred dollars. I gave Chester the check cashing fee for a week and an extra hundred for him. I didn't mention the keeper to him. Chester wouldn't know what the hell a keeper was any more than I had known a few hours ago.

Three hours or so after the keeper installed himself in my office, a marshal picked him up along with all the gear he brought with him.

The keeper wasn't really the enemy. He shook my hand when he left.

"Son, pay your taxes when they are due, or the state will send a person like me. The IRS will try to get it from your bank. If that doesn't work, they will demand that everyone walk out, then they will padlock your entrances and put up signs that the IRS has attached the premises."

"Thanks for the advice," I said. "I will not forget what you just told me." I was reeling with shock at the IRS extremes. What if they locked up the cash cow? I was more than grateful the keeper had given me fair warning.

The only person aware of what happened in real time was Susie. The way she handled the floor alone totally rocked. Meanwhile, Elena and I wrote out the checks for Chester and came up with a backup plan in case Chester couldn't give me the entire ten.

I gave my attorney two hundred dollars, and he was cool with that.

THE NEXT DAY, I told Elena, "I'm going over to Rene and cash a check, then head up to Vegas."

She didn't try to talk me out of it. She just looked concerned.

"Baby, what if you lose?"

I kissed her.

"I'm not a total loser." I don't know how reassuring that was, but she didn't comment.

I got eight thousand from Rene's Check Cashing and asked him if he could wait two days before he deposited the check. He charged me an extra fifty dollars for holding it. That gave me a week or more before the check would hit my bank.

19

VEGAS I CAN'T AFFORD TO LOSE

When I arrived in Vegas, I didn't go to the Tropicana. I had the taxi driver take me downtown. While it was just getting dark, I called Elena from a payphone in a casino called The Fremont. The taxi driver told me it was one of the older casinos built in the mid-fifties, but it had been remodeled a year or two ago. I wasn't there to check out the decoration, but it was splendid. I was as excited and anxious as you might expect.

"Susie is going to stay with me tonight," Elena said.

"I'm jealous," I said, but it was good to hear. It was good to have something to think about that was unrelated to the IRS and the keeper.

"Good luck, baby," she said.

I think that was the first time I went to Vegas determined that I needed to score. Like everyone else, I always wanted to win, but this trip was like I had to win or else. I don't know if that was good or not.

I was breaking a rule not to gamble on arrival, but I had no time. I still owed more to the State Board of Equalization and the

IRS. The possibility that the IRS could come into a space that was mine, throw us all out, and chain up my shop-it was overwhelming. All of Vegas was full of color, noise, crowds, and people hustling, but all I could think of was keeping a cool head and winning the game. The carpet was a crazy burgundy-gold-black patterned combo, just another note of chaos. I ignored the row of purple chairs parked in front of the crowded slots, picked a table, and waited for an empty seat. There was a crowd around the green felt table I chose. The wait calmed me down. The dealer was in a crisp white shirt.

I got an end seat. I liked getting the last cards, but I'm not the only one who does, so it wasn't always available. I had planned to buy a thousand in chips and slowly play twenty-dollar bets, hoping for continued luck. I sat down, reached in my pocket for the roll of hundreds I'd gotten from Rene, and counted out three thousand.

"Money plays," I said. I told myself I was not fucking afraid to lose the money. Fuck it. I was already buried. Another eight thousand wouldn't make much difference.

The pit boss smiled and repeated, "Money plays."

Pit bosses don't hang around to see how it goes. A passing waitress asked me if I wanted a drink. I asked for a coke—cold, no ice.

My two cards totaled twelve, and the dealer was showing a high card. I had to hit the twelve with the dealer showing a high card. He gave me a nine. Yes! The dealer had to draw a card. He also had twelve. He busted. I got paid in hundred-dollar chips. Three thousand big ones. I put my cash in my pocket. I ached to feel Elena behind me, patting my back with her knuckles softly like she did. I played a thousand and got a blackjack.

I played twenty dollars two times in a row and lost both times.

I had chips out, but I pulled the three thousand in cash I had put in my right pocket so as not to mix it with the roll from Rene.

"Money plays," I said.

"Money plays," the dealer said, "Three thousand."

The table was getting hot. I smiled at everyone. I didn't sweat the dealer having to shuffle before he finished passing out cards. I had twenty. Dealer had twenty. It was a push.

Next hand. "Money plays," I said again.

"Money plays," the dealer said.

I got a blackjack.

I was paid in chips. I put the cash away.

Before I took a sip of my Coke, I had won about fourteen thousand. I took all the chips and pushed them toward the dealer, who went through all my chips very professionally.

"Six thousand four hundred plays," he said.

The pit boss smiled and said, "Six thousand four hundred plays."

Dealer busted.

About three hours after arriving at the casino, I cashed in my chips and organized my cash. I put the eight thousand dollars in my left pocket—that was from Rene—and fifty-one thousand dollars in my right pocket.

As I was walking out, a man in a striped suit stopped me. He held a business card.

"My name is Joseph Graham. Please call me when you head back, and I'll fix you up with anything you need. I mean anything."

I reached in my pocket and came up with a hundred-dollar bill.

"Thanks, Joseph. My name is George Hatcher. I'd give you my card, but my pockets are filled with cash."

"Where you headed, George?"

"The airport."

"Give me five minutes, and I'll send you in one of our limos."

And so, I headed to the small Las Vegas airport and hoped there was an open flight back home. There was. A taxi delivered me from LAX to my apartment, where I found Elena on my bed. I guessed that Susie was in the other bedroom, but I was wrong. She was in the bathroom. She came out while Elena was kissing me like she hadn't seen me in ages. It was good to be home.

"Baby, I came back with the eight plus fifty-one thousand."

Elena was delighted. "I'm going to devour you. Your clothes, hurry."

"Give me ten to shower."

Elena said, "No shower."

Susie said, "No shower, Jefe."

The bedroom was dark but not pitch black. I could see them. Elena had a hungry look, like when everyone was gone from the shop, and we got in the back seat of cars and attacked each other. There was so much wrestling and playing around that it was much later when we finally had sex. I was more than relieved. I was happy.

IN THE MORNING, I called my accountant and attorney to come to the shop. Carlos asked if I had another keeper on my doorstep. I laughed, but it wasn't funny.

Donald, Carlos, Elena, and I went up to the office. Elena, Don, and Carlos took their seats on the sofa. I paced at first, then sat down and told them that the IRS had taken money from my account weeks ago. I showed them the reports I had mailed in without checks. I asked Don to figure out the numbers and then figure out how we can walk the payments due over in person. "I don't want to use mail," I said.

"I can do it," Donald said.

Carlos explained the deal he made with the State Board of Equalization the day before. I don't know how much of it was news to Donald, but at least it was relatively upbeat since my pockets weren't empty at the moment. I was eager to have the writ satisfied and the IRS off my back.

"I want to pay them all off today, and I want to pay the amount they haven't come after me for."

Elena and I went down to the shop floor to work. Elena was taking in a car when my attorney came down. We moved into the waiting area for a moment.

"Donald has the scoop on what I did yesterday and my number if he needs my feedback. He's up there figuring out what is due," Carlos said.

As I walked him to the entrance, I handed Carlos two hundred.

"Too much," he said.

I waved off his objections.

"It's okay, Carlos. The way you stopped everything, the way you attended to my emergencies. I appreciate it. You're a real trooper."

We said our goodbyes. I watched him take off at a fast pace for his office. When I turned back, I caught Elena staring at me. We weren't that far apart, but Jose was using some tool that was deafening. Elena's lips moved at me, but I didn't need silence to know she was saying, "I love you, George Hatcher."

I recently reflected on what love meant to my friend Elena and me back in the day when we were inseparable. It took me decades to see it clearly. Perhaps I understood it even then, but here it is now:

We both needed someone in our lives. We were learning the ropes of business together, craving companionship, yet neither of us wanted marriage. Love, for us, was defined by our mutual need for each other. We embraced our connection, sharing intimacy in our own unique way. Though we were open about exploring with others, our bond remained special. It was a distinct, profound love that thrived in our freedom and honesty.

By closing time, my accountant called me and said he had receipts for all money due IRS and State, including penalties and interest.

I deposited the money to clear Rene's eight thousand. When I got home, I parked myself at my kitchen dinette and called him to let him know he could deposit the check and that he didn't have to hold it. Elena had picked up steaks from the meat market, and they were sizzling on the stove. Potatoes were baking in the oven. Elena came over, gave me a kiss on the top of my head, and then checked the steaks.

"I owe you fifty dollars," Rene said.

"It's okay," I said.

"I'll credit you next time you are over."

"Thanks, Rene."

When he hung up, I saw dinner was still cooking. Elena was wearing nothing but a long t-shirt as she stood by the pan on the stovetop. She'd already pulled her rare steak, but mine needed to cook till it was gray, no matter what Jesse said. Anyway, I appreciated the view as she danced into the den to change the stack of records and danced back in. I had time to call Chester.

"Hey man, take those four checks you have and deposit them. They're solid gold."

"You the man," he said.

"No man. You the man."

I carried the phone into the living room, fed the fish, and saw that dinner was on the table when I got back in the kitchen.

Elena put out steak sauce, the knives that actually cut, then looked in my direction.

"I wasn't thinking," she said, looking at my hand. "How is your hand?"

"I was so worked up in Vegas I didn't even think of it. It's okay."

"Is that the hand you were..." She did a little cough and smiled.

"I used both of them," I said, remembering last night. "Did you forget?"

20

FINALLY SOMETHING FOR ELENA

I had money left over, and I knew where twenty-five hundred dollars of it was going. The dishes and plates were put away. We were lying on fresh linens. It felt like the right time to bring it up.

"I'd love to take you back to Acapulco. I should be able to do it, but it's like I'm trapped here, and you're trapped with me. It's not fair to you."

"If I feel trapped, I'll spring. Don't worry about me."

I kissed her.

"Elena, thank you for being here for me."

"Baby, do you really want to thank me?"

"Over and over again, thank you."

"Mm, I can think of another way." She put her mouth up to my ear and whispered as though we were not alone, "Go down there and do it to me. I'm so horny."

I kissed her before I worked my way down.

DURING OUR MORNING JOG, Elena brought it up just before the hill.

"G, you can't count on Vegas as your bailout every time."

"No way," I said. "I had to do it, but I'm not going back."

"Oh, baby, promise me."

I turned to look at her. "I promise."

WE DON'T USUALLY TAKE Sunday drives, but this Sunday, I drove us to Atlantic Boulevard, where all the car dealers are. I knew where we were going, but Elena didn't. It was the best surprise, and I was excited about it. I drove to a Ford dealership.

"Baby, what are we doing here?"

"I wanted to look at the new Mustang convertible up close."

"That's a hot car," she said. "I could cum without touching myself driving that car." It was inside the building behind the glass wall, glossy and its top down.

We reached the showroom. I opened the glass door to the dealership for her, and she ducked under my arm. A wine-colored convertible was inside, looking sexy as hell.

"To think you put two of these together," she said, laughing.

"It was the first model, not this one," I said.

A bell rang as we walked in, cueing a salesman to head in our direction, a guy twice our age.

"How do you like this color?" I asked.

"I'd fuck the salesman for it," she said, looking at the salesman. He turned beet-red but laughed.

She sat in the car.

"You look lovely in the driver's seat."

The salesman said, "It's Vintage Burgundy. Brand new car. Brand new color."

"Baby," I said. "Is this the color you love?" She was behind the wheel, checking it all out.

I whispered to the salesman, "I see the MSRP on the window. How much wiggle room you got?"

"Bud, these cars are selling for five hundred over sticker. If you want it, I can try and get the sales manager to give it to you for sticker plus taxes and license."

"Do it," I said.

I left her in the car, seriously mesmerized, and followed him to his office to write a check for twenty-five hundred eighty-eight dollars.[1] Before you wonder, the check was good. I felt fantastic that I could take that sliver from my Vegas winning and give Elena something she desired and deserved.

Those cars are still beautiful.

I DON'T KNOW if she caught the salesman saying something, or what, but she caught on that I had bought that car. Elena didn't make a scene or make the salesman blush. She took me aside and looked up at me. There was such a look in her eye.

"Are you planning to break up with me? Is that why you want me to have my own car?"

"Of course not."

She kept fishing. "How are you going to pay for it? I have money in the bank. You know that."

"Baby, I already wrote a check for it. Follow this man to his office. The car is going to be registered to you, and you will get the pink slip. It is your very own car."

"Why?"

"I'll tell you at home," I said.

---

1. $2,588 then comes to $21,522 dollars

While she was handling the paperwork, I called my insurance man, Jim. His card with all his numbers was in my wallet. Ramirez would have had a baby if he had any idea how much I paid for what Ramirez called 'stupid insurance.'

"Jim, sorry to bother you at home on a Sunday, but I'm calling about Elena. You know Elena?"

"Sunday is one of my biggest workdays," he said.

Maybe he was lying to put me at ease. Maybe it was true. He was still talking.

"...Sure, I know Elena, she works with you."

"She's buying a new Mustang straight off the dealer floor. I need a binder. Can you do it on a Sunday?"

"For you, anything you want, George."

"I'll have the sales guy give you what you need to bind, okay?" I was learning the jargon.

It took an hour to get it done. How long would it have taken if I had financed it like my Impala? A little longer, but not much. My credit was top drawer.

I followed Elena to Montebello Golf Course, where they had a Sunday brunch that went until four in the afternoon. We pulled into the parking lot and parked next to each other. We got out, and it was high drama like in the movies. We stood between our cherry cars and kissed for five minutes straight. I felt like Elena deserved more than a new car, but at the time, I couldn't handle anything. Some money guy in the movies, some rich guy like the Texan, would buy her a diamond or a Rolls-Royce to get her back.

We ate brunch, slowly savoring the feast without a drop of alcohol. We'd known each other a long time, but at the brunch, it was like we had just met. We stared at each other and fooled around with our food. It was a memorable afternoon, and the evening that followed was like a new beginning.

SATURDAY MORNING, right after our jog and before we hit the shower, the doorbell rang.

Elena and I looked at each other.

"Not again," I said to Elena.

"You aren't going over there this time. That fucker could shoot you."

Elena was behind me when I opened the door. It was Emma and Ava with big smiles. They each had two foil-covered plates.

"Emma cooked up a breakfast feast for you," Ava said.

I opened the door wide, and they went straight to put the plates on the kitchen table. Emma took the foil off and gave us the food tour.

"You have Denver omelets, bacon crisp like George likes it, and caramelized, almost burnt skillet potatoes like George prefers. Instead of toast, a stack of pancakes. The bottom two are stuffed with peanut butter."

"I don't know what to say," I said.

"Me neither. Thank you," Elena said and kissed Emma, then Ava.

"Love you, George," Ava said.

"Yeah," Emma said, "You're our hero."

"Sit down and eat," Emma said as they went through the doorway. "We're out of here. Need some sleep. My bed is calling my name." She gave a huge yawn, proving her point.

We walked into the kitchen and stared at the food, still in our jogging clothes and shoes.

"Shower or food?" Elena asked.

"I want food," I said.

"We're not even breakfast people, but that looks delicious. Was it Ava or Emma who was the cook?"

"Emma. At Denny's," I said.

"That was so nice of them, and right after, I said it was a bad idea to get involved or rescue them from that mad dog. I feel terrible."

"Eat. You'll feel better. I got dibs on one of the peanut butter pancakes."

"I got the other one," Elena said. "If my ass grows, don't bitch."

"I love your ass," I said. "Even if it grows."

"Yeah, like I'm going to believe that."

We munched along for ten minutes or so, plowing our way through the plates. I loved pancakes; actually, I still do.

Elena said, "I bet they take that bastard back."

"It's only a matter of time. They are all opportunists."

"How do you figure?"

"Ava and Emma know he produces clients. He needs to make bread from them. They're both taking advantage."

"I have a question, but you don't need to tell me," Elena said. She had knocked out one and a half pancakes and was on her omelet.

"I'll tell you," I said.

"Did you go down on them like you do me?"

"I would have, but neither let me do it."

"Why?"

"Your guess is as good as mine," I said. "Just so you know, both are squeaky clean."

"Baby, why you tell me that?"

"So, you know, that's all."

When we were done eating, we were too lazy to shower. I called Susie.

"We're taking today off. Please handle it with Alexa."

"I got it, Jefe. I'll taxi over there, and I won't be late."

"I'll reimburse you," I said.

"I dig being spontaneous. Now what?"

"I'm thinking you give me a ride to the beach in your cool convertible."

"I've got to put pads on my pussy if I'm going to drive that far."

"Oh, look who's gross now, I said.

"Baby, you're the scandalous one. I told you I cum driving the car. Also known as orgasm."

We laughed.

WE DIDN'T SHOWER. The jog sweat had dried up by the time we finished eating. Elena put the top down before she pulled out of her parking spot. When it was down, she screamed like I had pinched her or something. She was so happy. Then we hit the freeway to Santa Monica, then on Pacific Coast Highway to Malibu.

AT WORK, doing everything by the book caused shortages many times before the end of the month. I had over eighty thousand dollars in insurance receivables. Others in the same business would love to have the connections I had with adjusters and their companies. We were a one-stop shop for three companies. I didn't want to lose those connections. If only they all paid up like Farmers.

At Mike's, what we called the car wash shop, three cars a day became routine. Sometimes a bigger job came up that we handled at the main shop, so that was good. One bodyman was always working on a salvage car. I hired another bodyman to handle small bodywork that came up with a paint job or a walk-in that wanted a dent or scratch fixed. My payroll kept swelling.

I took Holmberg up on allowing me to overdraw my account. He would paychecks that came in even when there were insufficient funds. I would keep making daily deposits that quickly put me back in the black for a little while. When I wrote the bigger checks at the end of the month, I didn't push my luck and surprise Holmberg with a swarm of checks. I used Chester to give me the cash to deposit. Chester would hold the checks until I told him to clear them.

21

SAM KIND OF BAILS ME

After three breakfast meetings, I had my first lunch with Sam. They were all general meetings. He liked to stay in touch. We met at Canter's Deli, where we always ate breakfast. I guess Sam liked the fact that they kept a booth for him. I could understand why he liked the place. The gray-haired waitress always brought us coffee before we asked for it, put bread on the table, and remembered me enough to ask if I wanted a Denver Omelet.

Sam ordered a Reuben on sourdough with fries. I told Eunice, our waitress, that I'd have the same.

He complained about mechanics who didn't have Jose's work ethic.

I complained about the receivables I had from insurance companies.

"How much do you think they owe you right now?"

"Probably eighty thousand," I said.

"You know I have a small finance company?"

"Sure, you finance some of the salvage cars. Why?"

Eunice brought our sandwiches on hot white plates. Each

piece of sourdough bread was at least an inch thick, and there had to be two inches of corned beef plus another inch of sauerkraut. And there were enough fries on my plate for four people. I took a bite and found everything was delicious, but not surprisingly so. They had a lot of competition to beat out.

"Do you know what factoring is?"

"No, I don't know what factoring is, but Holmberg at my bank once told me that the bank doesn't factor or loan money on accounts receivable unless it's part of a package loan."

"Forget factoring," Sam said, adding more mustard to his sandwich. "I don't like it. I can buy the receivables you have, but it doesn't come cheap."

"Buy my receivables?"

"I write you a check for the accounts receivable you have at any given time, and when the money comes in, it's my money, not yours. If you did it with a bank familiar with your business, the bank would loan you money on your promise to turn the money over as the receivables come in. It gets complicated. I've done this a couple of times for other companies. You have an amazing business if you have that much paper."

"It is amazing, but I don't think I'm making any money."

"You got to be. To find out if you are making money, stop the expansion, settle for what you have." He drank his coffee and looked at me over glasses that sat low on his nose. "You're never going to stop expanding. If it's not in this business, it will be something else."

I sighed. It was true. I needed to expand.

We both reached for napkins from the silver box under the window. I rested the heel of my hand on mine. Sam dabbed a spot of mustard off his mouth.

"What companies owe you?"

I told him Farmers was great because the customer had a

check to pay me soon after the car was finished, and he or she was satisfied with the work.

"There is a risk in everything when it comes to financing," Sam said. "Your paper is low-risk. I have paper in other businesses that don't always work very well, and I take a loss. I have to compensate for it by doing what I do and charging for it."

"If I get on the phone and hammer the companies, I can probably spring five thousand at a time without waiting, and I even send for the checks. That gets old. I don't like it. They don't like it. And it makes me look weak."

"I don't know that I would buy receivables ongoing, but if you have eighty thousand worth, I'll charge you twenty percent and give you the money. I won't do what a bank or finance does. I am not going to type up an assignment for each claim stating that I own the money owed to you, and it's not owed to you but to me."

"I'll add it up. I'll take eighty percent just this time," I said. I was uncertain if I was making twenty percent on the work, but it would give me some breathing room.

"Okay, here is the deal. Make a copy of each claim owed to you, bring them over tomorrow, and I'll give you a check for eighty percent of their face value. You sign a simple note for the money I give you, and every time you deposit an insurance check that I bought, you send me a check over for the full amount, letting me know what claim you are paying off."

"Deal," I said. "Thank you, Sam."

"Between now and tomorrow, if you have second thoughts, no problem, no hard feelings, kid. You know I love you."

We finished eating. Sam finished his. Not a crumb left on his plate. Eunice brought me a box, and I put half of my sandwich and a mother lode of fries in it. Elena had skipped lunch so I could leave the shop, so I knew she'd appreciate it.

We got up. He gave me a hug that lifted me off the ground. Sam was a hefty guy.

On my way to the shop, I wanted to be happy about the deal I made, but I was having trouble. Maybe it's the Libra in me.

I shook hands on the deal, so even though he said I could back out. I didn't do it. A deal's a deal. I wanted to be the guy who lives up to every deal. Chester, Rene, and the check cashing places that Mike had found gave me whatever I asked for, not because I paid them, but because they trusted me. I'd known Holmberg at my bank for years. He had confidence in me. This was important.

When I have a heart-to-heart with myself, I always look back and think about the trust I breached, fucking up the oath I took when I enlisted in the Navy. My first and second divorces were not entirely my fault. My third divorce was still upcoming. It was impossible to say it was my fault or hers. We were both too young, I think. And I had not counted on marrying her family.

I gave Elena her sandwich. She went upstairs to eat by herself while I watched the floor, but as soon as she came down, I asked Alexa to come over and work the rest of the afternoon with Susie. Elena and I went home. We were taking turns with the cars. One day, we took her car, and the next day, my car. She was driving the Mustang today because of the lunch meeting with Sam.

"Is something wrong?" Elena asked.

"Not at all. I had a good meeting with Sam. We made a deal on something I'm iffy about. I need peace and quiet to mull it over. I can't back out of it. I mean, I can, but I can't do it in good conscience. I need to know for myself if I made a mistake."

"Gee, G…" she laughed. "Did you catch that, gee, G?"

I laughed to let her know I caught it.

"So, what is the deal?"

I told her about trading the receivables for eighty percent of their value.

"Before we left the shop, I ran a total of the open claims we haven't been paid. It's eighty-one thousand five hundred. I was almost right on. I told him eighty thousand."

"How much would a bank charge for the same thing?"

"My bank doesn't do that kind of stuff."

"Baby, that's a lot of bread in one lump."

"I haven't even figured if I even made a profit on the jobs."

"You did."

"Why do you say that?"

"You approved the estimates the adjuster put together or wrote your own estimate."

"Good point. So, you'd say the worst thing is that I gave up the profit?"

"I don't know that. Hopefully, you made more than twenty percent profit. When my aunt or brother sells a casket, and let's say we pay four hundred for it, we sell it for a thousand. Very little to figure out. Car crash repairs are not coffins."

I laughed so hard it made her laugh, and she pulled over to the curb.

We stopped by the store and picked up a Tab before we got to the apartment.

Elena got the ice out, and I opened the Tab. We were trying the Coke product Tab for the second time to see if it tasted better than when we tried it before.

It didn't, but we brought our icy Tabs into the living room and sat down with them anyway.

"So, how does it work?"

She sat on the edge of a hardback chair facing me. I was sitting on one of the stuffed chairs.

I explained, "He writes me a check for eighty percent of whatever I am selling him. He trusts me. He doesn't take anything, but he wants a copy of each claim. When we get paid on a claim, I put the insurance check in my business account and write Sam a check immediately, which he then credits my advance."

"Sounds easier than running to Chester."

"I have a feeling I'm always going to need a Chester in my life. I brought home this much money from Vegas, and it went in a heartbeat."

"Part of it went to buy my car. I told you not to."

"Elena, please. That was the best money I ever spent."

She immediately moved on my lap. There were kisses and other perks.

"You are the most generous person I ever met," she said.

"Not true. The Texan gave you five thousand when you left Hawaii."

"He should have given me ten times that for using my vajayjay for six months."

She laughed first.

"Anyway, I can't back out."

"Why do you say you can't back out?"

"I shook hands on the deal. Look, I don't regret it. The idea is just new to me. He's making twenty percent just because he can afford to wait a month or two."

"G, you know they take longer sometimes."

I heard a noise outside and got up to look out the window. It was a spectacularly sunny day in the middle of the week, and the pool was deserted. The water looked wonderful, and the inside of the pool was sparkling blue. There were plenty of chaises to lie on, and the way the palm trees looked in the sunlight was seductively tropical.

"Let's get in the pool," I suggested. "I love getting home early like this."

"How would you know? We never get home like this."

"I'm going to fuck you, Elena."

"Before or after the swim?"

"Before, during, and after."

"Your neighbors are going to love that," she said.

THE NEXT DAY I drove to Sam's shop with eighty-one thousand five hundred worth of claims. He barely looked them over, although I was sure he would. Sam wanted me to know he trusted me. He knew he could make money with me or off me. Sam became a dear friend. I learned a lot from him.

"I know you have a good relationship with your bank, but if you want, I'll call Kitty at my bank and tell her to set you up in case you ever need another bank."

I couldn't imagine I would ever need another bank. My bank account at Holmberg's had been around since I was mowing lawns for small change.

"Sure. I can open the account with your check."

I met Kitty, who was thirtyish, and way too young and pretty to be the manager of a big branch like she was.

"Sam didn't tell me how pretty you are," I said.

Kitty smiled and said, "He told me you were just out of high school, a real sixteen going on thirty kind of boy, and real cute. He was right. Don't worry, I know you're not sixteen." She reached over and almost touched my head but drew back without contact. "Look at that hair. I love it."

"Um. Thanks?"

"I'll give you a receipt for the check you are opening the account with," she said. "And I'll give you some temporary checks. Tomorrow when you come to take me to lunch, bring your corporate seal and a copy of your articles of incorporation. You know what that is?"

"I know. I'll bring it. What time?"

Something about her reminded me of Alicia or maybe

Elena. Maybe it was her teeth. They were very white, and her incisors were noticeably sharp. "Noonish," she said.

"Where you want to eat?"

"Have you been to Nicolas in City of Commerce?"

"I've been there," I said. "You know they model topless, right?"

"I like it," she said.

We shook hands, and I left.

I went through the door into the daylight. When I reached the sidewalk, I turned to look back at the bank. It was easily twice the size of Holmberg's branch. What would her customers think if they ran into her at Nicolas? Maybe she liked girls. That was okay with me, though in the early sixties, being gay was not accepted. But I definitely didn't get that vibe from her. Kitty was not gay.

I looked at the receipt. Sixty-five thousand two hundred dollars.

Before turning the ignition, for a moment, I thought about how much I could make in Vegas with that much money to play with.

I got back to the shop a little before three.

Elena made a file for Eagle Finance and included a copy of the check he gave me in it.

"Did you sign anything?" she asked.

"He was busy. He handed me a blank paper and a pen and told me to put a date at the top and write, 'I promise to pay Eagle Finance the sum of eighty-one thousand five hundred dollars no later than one year from today.' I signed it."

"That's all?"

"That's it."

"But he only gave you $65,100. Why the $81,500?"

I frowned because I thought she'd understood. "Baby, I gave him eighty-one thousand five hundred in claims. As the checks come in, I will pay him, and he will give me credit on the eighty-one thousand five hundred."

"I knew that. Just wanted to be sure." She stuck her tongue out at me.

"Stick it out again. I want to bite it."

I PULLED Alexa from Eastland II to work with Susie. Elena and I went home early again. We headed to the car. We were in the Impala today. I drove.

"Are you happy with Sam's deal?"

I sighed. "There went all my receivables. There go my excuses, up in smoke. Now I got nothing to blame when I run short. It's true. It's not just me. Every month that I'm short, we all blame the insurance accounts receivables for the shortage."

"Baby, until you stop doing insurance work, you will have accounts receivable. You also have too many employees and are too careless with electricity. I see drains everywhere."

"Once I hire someone, I can't just fire them."

"Yes, you can."

"What else is wrong?"

"It's only my opinion," Elena said, "and it's nothing I haven't said before."

"You mean like paying my key people a lot more than a good salary?"

"Yes."

"I know I don't pay you nearly enough," I said. "I must be crazy."

"I'm good," she said.

"I'm going to give you a raise."

"You see? There you go."

We laughed.

We got to my apartment. I opened the fish food and put my hand near the top of the water holding a batch of flakes. The fish came rushing to the top to scarf down the pinch of food.

I looked up from the tank and saw Elena was already in a string bikini.

"I can get used to coming home early like this," she said.

"Baby, I can count your pubic hair from here. Is that what you really want to wear? Maybe the suit you wore yesterday?"

"No one is out there. Besides, you cannot see my pubic hair." She laughed at me and shoved me toward the bedroom to change.

As she had said, no one else was there. We had the pool to ourselves. Everyone was probably at work except for Ava and Emma, who were probably still in bed.

"What are you going to do with the money?" Elena got on her back and floated. She had her eyes closed, and the sun cast a dark shadow of her eyelashes across her face. She looked so beautiful and so relaxed.

"Coast for a couple months and maybe open another shop."

"No. Please, no." Elena sat up and sank into the water. It was only for a second. She popped above the surface, spitting water, sputtering, still saying, "No."

I grinned. I didn't have a place in mind, but would I roll the dice again to help the overall cash flow? Yes. I glimpsed the solution. What I failed to see is that I needed another spray booth and oven in the main shop. And I could have the room for it if I were to kick out the mechanic, the upholstery guys, and the two bodymen who did my insurance wrecks. We had more than ten customers a day wanting to paint their cars, but our capacity was ten. A sure cure had been in my face for a long time, but I was stubborn.

∾

ONCE A MONTH, Donald was again coming to write all checks, including taxes, and then it was up to me when I mailed everything out.

"That damn Sam. He's everywhere," Donald said. "I didn't know you knew him, but I should have guessed."

"Don't you like him? I sure do."

"I never met him, but the shops I handle all owe him and buy from him. He's like a company store."

"He bought more than eighty thousand in receivables from me for sixty-five thousand. What do you think?"

"Twenty percent. No one will do it for less, and Sam just does it, no bull. He must like you. It's a lot of money."

I thought of the handwritten IOU.

"It was fast," I said. "He told me to get an account with First Interstate. Sam referred me over there."

"Good bank. Good backup. Smart move."

"Coast," Donald said. "Don't take any chances going to Vegas. You're way ahead."

"I'm not going to Vegas," I said.

I left Donald in the office and walked downstairs to the shop floor.

22

KITTY THE BANKER

Lunch with Kitty was a trip. It's hard to know much of a body if you dress like a bank manager. I was pretty sure Kitty had a great shape, but it was just a guess. She had short kittenish hair but was tall, like what Elena called a bouffant, and wore suits that hid more than they suggested and jackets with important-looking lapels. She was feminine, but she talked like a man, a banker. I mean, she was not manly, but she could handle herself in a room of male suits. Anyway, she and I were fully dressed at the table, and our server was just wearing panties.

At Nicolas, the City allows the restaurant to have models. The models could be topless but not bottomless. Years later, the eatery would become an upper-class, expensive strip club with both top and bottom off. Those days, it was tops off only.

"Who is enjoying this more, you or me?" Kitty asked as a model left our table.

"Hey, I dig it," I said to Kitty. "Do you?"

"I like to see the looks when the model comes up to the table."

I smiled. "Yeah, it's funny."

Kitty was not the only woman there. The nudity didn't seem to bother her. And she'd suggested having lunch at this place. So I figured I was in the clear of any blame.

"You married?"

"I'm about to be divorced," I replied.

"I'm sorry."

"No, don't be sorry. We both want it."

"You're so young to be going through this."

"Kitty, I'm not going through anything. I have my own apartment. I have a life, and so does she. We have a beautiful daughter. We're on good terms."

"You're adorable," she said, leaning toward me.

I gave her a look. Adorable are puppies and kittens.

"Are you married?"

"My husband is married," she said. "I'm not."

WE WENT to the bank in my car. She took what she needed to open the account. I picked out the checks I wanted, a different color from the ones from Holmberg's bank. The starting check number was five thousand. When I got up to leave, she gave me a light kiss on my lips. I had not met anybody like her in my decades of dealing with banks.

Sam had brought the branch a lot of business. She had been promoted fast. I don't know if there was a connection. If having Kitty as manager kept Sam's bank balances looking good, Kitty had solid job security.

Donald had come to do the books. He was about to leave.

"With what you have in the bank," Donald said, "you need another fourteen thousand to cover the checks I left to mail."

"I'll handle it," I said.

I figured it would be easy. I would just move that shortage from Kitty's bank to Holmberg's, and that would be it for the month. It seemed like I should do something with the money I got from Sam. After all, I paid a premium of sixteen thousand dollars. I kept telling myself it was business.

We were at home. It was after work, nothing was pressing, the paper plates from dinner were in the trash, a movie was playing on the television, and Elena and I were sprawled out on the couch. I ought to be relaxed. The bills were up to date. Everything was going ok. Donald and Sam had warned me to forget about extending the business and just keep it going at this level for now.

"Be happy for once," Elena said. "Be content."

"Baby, I am happy." I tried making a funny face. Not sure if it bombed. Elena changed the subject, sort of.

"Should we bring Susie home with us tomorrow? Will that make you happy?" Elena asked.

"I got you. Everything I want is built-in Elena."

She kissed me.

"You want me to ask her or not?"

I looked up at the ceiling like I was thinking about it.

Elena put her arms around my waist and tightened.

"Well?"

"Have her come Friday after work and stay overnight. That way, you and I can take off tomorrow and have a long weekend."

That got me a big hug and a big kiss.

"I love you," she said

"Tell me the truth. Do you have Susie over for me, or do you do it because you dig it, too?" I asked.

"I like her company. The three of us are fun together."

"Baby, anything else?"

"Yeah. I dig what we do in bed together." A big smile showed up on her face. "I'm human."

"That's important to me."

"You know I'm not gay." Elena giggled.

"I know, and Susie isn't gay," I said.

"I agree, G. Any other questions?"

"Nope. I'm a happy camper."

I FELT like Elena was getting worn out. I was getting worn out, but I couldn't cave. I was needed at work, sometimes everywhere at once. The exhaustion was getting to me, and I had no one to admit it to. Elena always had my ear. She had me to admit it to, but she never did.

THAT NIGHT, we watched The Untouchables and wound up on the couch like a couple of spider monkeys. I had a jar of peanut butter and a spoon, and she had a pint of ice cream. She was spooning to herself and, once in a while, to me. I reached up to the lamp on the end table and switched it off. We were settled in, shaking off the remains of the day. It was good. The lights were out except for the flashes of the television, and we were ticking slower and slower like a couple of wind-up dolls at the end of the day. At that time, only one or two channels had their programming in color. Both my televisions were color. The color television Sophia and I had from the start, she kept.

"Is this what married people do?" Elena asked.

"I never got far enough in my marriages to know."

Elena pinched me.

"Ouch."

"You were with your present wife longer than the others. You said you lived down on 8th Street and watched TV a lot. It was so small you couldn't invite anyone over."

I laughed. "Honey, you would not believe how small that apartment was."

"I do know. You told me."

"Marriage messes up everything," I said.

Our faces met in the dark. Light washed over us as Elliot Ness walked through a long-ago black-and-white Chicago day. I could see myself reflected for a moment in Elena's eyes.

"I don't want to marry you, but I never want to leave you," she said.

I have a habit of taking big breaths and exhaling slowly enough that no one would notice what I was doing. When she said that, I was just about to inhale. I stopped.

"I feel the same way," I said.

"You said you married your first wife because you thought that was the only way to have her for good."

"I was barely seventeen," I said.

"Nah. You were forty, at least. You were seventeen when you were nine."

I started to laugh and smothered her with kisses so she would stop talking about me and my marriages.

"Should I freeze what's left of the ice cream?" I asked, snatching the carton.

I gave her a hand and pulled her lazy ass off the sofa. I headed to the kitchen with the carton.

"Are you kidding? We ate it all." She giggled.

I looked into the empty carton, not that there was much to see in the dark, and tossed it. We collided on the bed.

I rubbed her stomach lightly. She was fit. The jogging made us both fit.

"Are you glad Susie is coming over tomorrow?"

"Not if you're not."

"I asked you first."

"Rub me lower," she said, "until I go to sleep."

I slipped my hand down below the sleep shirt she was wearing.

"I'll pass if you want," I said. "I got all this," I touched her where she liked.

"Baby, keep your hand there... yeah."

ON MONDAY, Elena was downstairs on the floor. I was in my office. The desk drawer that used to hold all those unsent reports was remarkably clean. I called Kitty at the bank.

"Hey, you," she said after I told her who I was.

"A quick question."

"Shoot."

"I'm not pressed for money right now, and I figure the best time to set up a loan is when a person is not drowning."

Kitty laughed. "Shoot. What are you looking for?"

"My bank where I've been forever will loan me whatever I need when I need to buy equipment, and they give me the courtesy of paying my checks if I'm overdrawn. When that happens, I cover the shortage right away, but it's like a loan. The problem, if it is a problem, is when I need a short-term unsecured loan, I can't get it."

"How much?"

"I'm just fishing, like I said. I'm cool right now."

Through the phone, I could hear a tapping sound in her office and realized she was drumming her nails on the desk. I'd seen her do this in time to the music when I'd taken her to lunch, and maybe it was something she did when she was thinking.

"Sounds like you want a line of credit, and when you need money, you draw down on that line."

"Yeah, that's it."

"How do you look on paper?"

"My credit is good. I had some past due taxes, but I paid up. My car is paid off. I have no personal debts that I can think of. Is that what you mean?"

"Do you have an accountant?"

"I do. He's a CPA. His office is two blocks away from me."

"Tell him to prepare a year-to-date p & l and a balance sheet, and you drop it off whenever you want. I'll do something for you."

"Wow, just like that?"

"Sam says you're a prince."

"Me, a prince?" I laughed a long time over that one.

IT WAS a gray day that looked like rain, but I walked to Donald's office to pick up the papers.

"It looks good," Donald said. "You're lucky to have good credit. Put that with how you look on paper, and you're a candidate for a bank loan."

I ran the docs straight to my new bank. Actually, I drove, but I stood with sweaty palms in Kitty's office while she accepted the folder. I felt like I was pulling the wool over everyone's eyes. People kept coming into her office, and her phone was constantly ringing. She was busy and told me she'd give me a call when she had a chance to look over everything. At that moment, it was a good thing that I did not need a line of credit. The sweaty palms were a reaction to doing something I had not done before applying for a standby line of credit from a big bank like Kitty's. Ever since we met, Holmberg had always made it easy for me, whether I needed a car loan or an equipment loan.

It was still early when I got back to the office, and I was on pins and needles for an hour or so before she called back. Then the phone rang, and I got the news.

Kitty agreed with Donald.

"I'm going to set you up with a ten-thousand-dollar line of credit," Kitty said. "When you need an advance, you call in, and the operations officer or anyone on the platform will deposit what you want into the checking account we have open for you. How's that?"

"Kitty, thanks. It's a great start for me."

"There is more where that came from as long as you pay up when a payment is due."

"I owe you," I said.

"I'll take you up on that," she said. "We'll set up lunch after I get back from vacation. I will send out the documents in the mail to you today. When you have them signed, drop them off. I'm going to take a week off, but the line will be set up as soon as you bring back the documents."

I was so energized by the confidence Kitty threw my way that I called Elena on the intercom.

"Come up to the office."

It wasn't even lunchtime.

As soon as she walked in, she took one look at me and said,

"What? Why are you so red?" She dropped her clipboard on my desk. Her expressions were so vivid that I could practically read her mind. I knew she was wondering what was so important that I pulled her off the floor. She glanced at the sofa and back to me. I guess we were both transparent to some degree. She closed the door. "What is it?"

"Kitty gave me a line of credit. A ten-thousand-dollar line of credit."

"Neat." She grinned at me impishly. "Why so little?"

"Little? Ten thousand is little?"

She rolled her eyes and laughed at me. "Is it possible you called me up here to celebrate?"

"Damn straight," I said. "I called you up here to, you know what."

"What is that?"

"You know."

"I don't know what you mean, Mister."

I walked around my desk and hugged her, my hands cupping her ass.

"Oh, you mean you want to fuck me?"

"Yes," I said. "You are the hottest woman on earth."

She made a noise halfway between a snort and a laugh. "I'm supposed to believe that after the way you did Susie last weekend, and you spent all night with her without me there?" She pushed me back a little so she could look at me. "It's going to cost you."

I smiled.

"How much?"

"What's the going rate with Ava and Emma?"

"Baby, no," I said, "Don't say that."

"Okay then, a free sample."

"Much better."

I pulled her to me so that our bodies were touching pelvis to pelvis and all the way up. I felt her right hand let go of my ass while she locked the door one-handed, then returned without ever breaking our kiss.

"So talented," I said into her mouth. "You are the hottest woman on earth."

23

HERE I GO AGAIN

I found the perfect spot on Whittier Boulevard, owned by the biggest towing company in East Los Angeles. The city disallowed long-term storage of impounded vehicles on the boulevard so they had to get a location where they could get the permits. The big building was made-to-order, almost identical to my gold mine shop on Brooklyn and Rowan. The theater across the street was probably the biggest and busiest in the area. On the corner was a former office building owned by an Armenian. I pictured it as a fast-food place. Tacos. I guess I have a good imagination. I could practically taste those tacos.

"You can have the entire property for fifteen hundred a month," the Armenian said on our third meeting. "If you want to rent out part of it, I don't care. You take it as is where is. I pay nothing for repairs. Pretend the property belongs to you."

"You are killing me," I said for the thousandth time.

"George, you have the huge yard with the fence covered from the Boulevard. Imagine all the work you can do outside. The city won't care. They only want me out of there because the lot was like a pregnant woman in her tenth month. It was filled with cars."

"I know the story. If I take it, how many months are you going to throw in for the improvements I plan to make?"

The bastard smirked at me.

"Not a single month. I said to pretend it is your property. If I had a buyer, the property is worth five hundred thousand. You can't buy it for fifteen hundred a month."

"You don't have a buyer. You have me, and I'm interested."

SAM LOVED THE PLACE. He thought I could make a lot of money there, but I'd have to do bodywork, paint, and high-volume insurance work.

"You should do some serious thinking before jumping in, no matter how good it is. If you do it, put a mechanic in there like Jose at the other place."

"You'll buy the receivables?" I asked him.

"I think we could come to an understanding, yes," he said.

HOLMBERG TOLD me if it was him, he would wait.

KITTY SAID expansion was exciting but didn't offer an opinion. Nor did she offer me any money. I had not used the line of credit at her bank, but I had used more than half of the money Sam traded me for the receivables he bought from me.

My team knew the place. Everyone knew the tow truck company. They had the city and county contract for towing cars a tremendous square mile that covered practically all of the East Los Angeles area. That had been headquarters for years.

"It's going to cost you big time to do there what you did here," Elena said.

"I'm not moving fast on this one."

"Baby, wait. Don't do it yet. What if Sam decides not to buy the receivables? Think of the payroll and parts you need to buy to make a place like that work."

I had the idea in my head. I could see it all.

"I think a taco place could do great. I asked Chris and Jess about it."

"I know," Elena said, "and they said it's going to cost you to make it a restaurant. It was an office. Besides, baby, you aren't a restaurant person."

"Why can't I be?"

I wasn't going to do the cooking. I figured that my buddies Chris and Jess would help me jump-start the place.

Donald told me, "George, this place is too big."

Carlos said, "You need to be the decision maker. I suggest you form a different corporation if you proceed."

"Why?"

"If something happens, if it goes belly up, you don't go down the tubes with it. Too many eggs in one basket."

"Makes sense," I said. "If I decide to go with it, I'll think of a name."

Elena shook her head and wagged her finger at me. She saw rough weather ahead. "Every day since you came up with this crazy notion, I've prayed that the Armenian would rent it to someone else.

"Baby, I never knew you prayed. We've never talked religion."

"I pray. I just don't make a fuss out of it," she said.

And then later that day at the shop, around three pm, I knew what I was going to do.

"Sweets," I told Elena. "It's you and Susie here. I'm off to Vegas."

She frowned at me. A thundercloud of a frown.

"Ouch," I said.

"Ouch, my ass," she said. "You promised."

"I have an itch. I need to do it. I'm going to pick up eight thousand from Rene and just drive up. Let me drive you to the apartment to get your car."

"I'll take a taxi and take Susie with me."

I kissed her right there on the shop floor. She looked me up and down, touched my hair, picked a bit of lint off my shoulder.

"You didn't even pack. Are you going like that?"

I was in my usual jeans and shirt, which I'd worn all day. "I can always buy a t-shirt if I mess this up."

"Baby, no," she said, frustrated with me.

Susie gave us space. It was after three, when customers would be coming in to pick up their cars, and the waiting room would be filling up.

"I love you," I said.

"You don't love me. If you did, you wouldn't go."

I put my hands on her shoulders and then one finger to lift her sinking chin. I met her eyes, hoping to see some confidence looking back at me.

"Don't say any more, or you'll mess up the positive I've got inside."

She sighed, rubbed my hair, and managed a smile that lifted my spirits.

"Don't drive fast," she said.

I walked past Susie out front. She did a fancy wave to me with her fingertips, and I read her lips.

"Good Luck."

Elena was worried I'd blow what I had left at Kitty's bank. I pretended I didn't have that money. That's why I got the cash from Rene Check Cashing like it made any difference. I wrote the check from my account at Holmberg's Bank, where I didn't have eight thousand. Crazy thinking.

24

VEGAS I'M BACK

I could have called the host who gave me a card from the Fremont, or I could have called a host who put us in a suite twice at the Flamingo, but I didn't. When they know you are coming, there's too much pressure. I never called ahead, but I felt that way.

The whole way there, I argued with myself where I'd be going. I'd come first to the Flamingo. To get to the Fremont, I'd have to go downtown.

I went to the Flamingo.

Not even an hour after Valet took my car, I was at a table. I broke the rule.

∼

I HAD LEFT Rene's Check Cashing about three-thirty and headed straight to the freeway. I arrived at the Flamingo at about eight. I didn't call Elena, walked around a little bit, and sat down about 8:30.

The eight thousand I got from Rene was in my right pocket. I already had about three hundred in cash. It was in my left pocket.

I watched a table for a few minutes, and I liked it. The one vacant seat was in the middle. I didn't like being in the middle. I nodded hello to the lady on my right and a guy on my left. The lady was playing with ten-dollar chips. The guy had a stack of chips in three colors. They were both dressed fancier than I was, but I wasn't here for a fashion show. The dealer's tag said 'Jane' and under her name, Alabama. Alabama was blonde, very fair, light eyes. Very heavy makeup, but I figure that's part of the job.

"Hi, Alabama," I said.

She smiled. "Are you in?"

I reached in my right pocket, pulled out the cash, and put it on the table.

"Money plays," I said. "Should be eight thousand there."

"Money plays," she called out. She counted. "Eight thousand."

"Money plays eight thousand," the pit boss said and walked away. He looked familiar.

The dealer stayed at eighteen. I showed a blackjack. The other players at the table got riled up. I kept my cool.

I took one of the hundred-dollar chips and tossed it over to Alabama. She smiled, took the chip, tapped it on the table, and put it in her shirt pocket.

"Thank you."

I took the eight thousand from the table and put it back in my right pocket.

She gave me all hundred chips. I played slowly at first. A hundred a hand. Anything interesting, I would double down.

My stack was getting bigger. No one had left the table, and the dealer was getting terrible hands, but I knew that would change.

I took the eight thousand out of my pocket again.

I put the cash in front of me. Alabama smiled. She had to know I liked playing with green cash, and her smile told me she knew.

"Money plays if it's okay," I said.

"It's fine," she said.

"Money plays." She counted. "Eight Thousand."

"Money plays eight thousand," the pit boss repeated.

I knew I was rushing it. I knew Alabama's luck would change against all of us.

She busted. She paid the table and paid me eight thousand. I tossed another hundred at her.

When she smiled, I saw teeth.

I had a mountain of chips in front of me.

"Can I change colors on part of your chips?" she asked.

"Sure," I said. "Give me thousands."

I really wasn't paying attention to the players around me. They brought me down. They seemed stressed for me or happy about their winnings. I didn't want to look at them. I did look at Alabama. She was a very pretty girl, but not my type. Come to think of it, what girl is my type?

I thought of Elena right off.

Alabama went to dinner and returned. She was having a bad night, and when she came back, her luck changed. That's when I left the table, a little after midnight. Alabama had seven hundred-dollar chips from me, and her relief had one chip. I left the table with seventy-seven thousand dollars.

I CALLED Elena for the first time since I got to Vegas.

"Baby, it's okay if you lost. Come home."

I laughed. I tried hard not to tell her. I wanted to wait until I got home, but I couldn't do that.

"Oh my God, no!"

"What do you mean, no?"

"I mean, Yes, it's fantastic. Oh, I should have gone with you. It's too late. You can't drive back now. Get a room."

"I'm going to go pee and head home," I said. "Fix it so we don't work tomorrow."

"You mean today."

"Right, today."

"I'm going to worry about you driving back after the drive up."

"I'm good, baby."

I saw the sunrise as I arrived in Monterey Park and parked in my spot next to Elena's car. That's when the craziness hit me. I started to laugh. I put the key in the door and ran up the stairs. Elena and Susie were already up.

Elena devoured me with kisses like she did. Susie watched.

Then it was Elena's turn to watch as Susie did her thing on me. The thing with Susie wasn't just a sex thing. We dug her company. Elena really liked her. Elena had left her friends behind when she moved in with me. Like me, she had no social life. I don't think I pushed her to be with me constantly as we were, but I would have been a nut case without her.

The smell of the coffee was an aphrodisiac.

After the coffee and a shower, we went to work. "We can take off the weekend," I said.

"Outta sight," Elena said.

25

ANOTHER SHOP

Once I got to the office, I did the math. I had never been as cash flush as that morning.

"I have forty-five-thousand left at Kitty's bank, not counting the line of credit. With what I won yesterday, that's almost a hundred-twenty-five-thousand big ones. Fuck."

"That's a lot of coffins," Elena said with a chuckle. "Baby, coast for a while."

"I am," I said.

∼

I FELT like I needed to share my good fortune, so I drove over to see Mike and gave him three thousand.

"I figure I owe you. Had you not turned me on to Vegas, I would have never gone there to gamble."

Mike grinned. "You rock, G. Thanks, bunches!" He stretched his hand for a handshake. I gave a hundred each to the workers there. I drove over to Soto and gave Gil three hundred and the workers one hundred each. When I was done,

I returned to Eastland, where I found Elena frowning and anxious.

"What's wrong, baby?"

"It's almost two, and I haven't eaten."

"I'm sorry," I told Elena where I'd been. "I lost track of time." I waved to Susie, who was just returning from the meat market. "You guys doing okay?"

Susie was just getting back from lunch.

"Let's go order," Elena said, hauling me by the hand in the direction of the meat market. "I'm so hungry I can hear my stomach growling louder than Jose's power tools."

"Really?" Halfway there, I stopped, which also stopped Elena. We were in the parking lot, twenty feet from the meat market entrance. "Let me listen," I said, putting my ear to her tummy. I listened for a few seconds, then started hauling Elena toward the entrance. "You better get some food in there quick," I said. "Sounds like a zoo in there."

After we ate, I distributed cash to my team at the cash cow shop where Elena and I worked.

I gave Susie five hundred.

"Jefe, a hundred is totally cool. This is too much."

"Take the money," I said with a growl. A friendly growl.

I tried to give Elena three thousand. It was in an envelope. "Baby, don't be stupid. I'm not taking it. No!"

At home that night, I kept pushing her to take the money. "I'm going to get totally pissed at you if you reject this gift from me. You do so much for me. I need to give you something before it's gone."

"G, this is more than my car cost you. No."

Finally, we compromised. She agreed to take two thousand.

"Baby, please stop giving money away. Save it. There will be a rainy day ahead." Then she said. "Are you giving Ava and Emma some?"

"Thanks for reminding me," I said with a grin. Elena whacked my shoulder as she does. "You better stop with the giving."

A day or so after, I gave Ava and Elena a thousand each. They both cried. I was so happy I almost cried.

When Elena found out. "G, stop it already!"

"I didn't have to tell you," I said.

"I wish you hadn't told me." Then she said. "G, it's your money."

"They have to do a whole bunch of tricks to make two grand," I said. "I'm happy I was able to do it."

Eventually. "Promise the giving money away is done with."

"I need to give my parents a little and Sophia. After that, I promise."

WITH THE GIFTING out of the way, the shop deal I wanted was back on the table.

"One last try," I told Elena. "I promise. If I don't get an acceptable deal on lower rent, I'm done."

"Good luck," she said, crossing her fingers and holding them even with her ears. I left the shop for the last-ditch effort to work the rent lower. I returned from Vegas a few days before.

"George, I'm not moving from fifteen hundred. No time to negotiate. Take it or leave it."

"Hear me out for just a minute," I said.

"I'm listening."

"Fifteen hundred a month is eighteen thousand for the year, right?"

"A steal for you. Yes, it's eighteen thousand. Why?"

"I'll give you twelve thousand right now. Advance rent for a year."

"No."

"Give me the number that you will accept. Rent for an entire year."

He looked at me. Silence.

"Seventeen thousand," he said.

I was done. I got up, not bluffing.

"I promise not to bother you again on this." I was at the door.

"George, come back here and sit down."

I gave him fifteen thousand in cash. He gave me a receipt for twelve months' rent paid in advance. We agreed to write up a five-year lease within a week. He agreed that I had the right to bail on the lease at the end of the first twelve months, but if I stayed one day over, I was bound for the remaining four years.

"Rent starts today," he said. He put his hand out for a handshake.

I intended to go to battle for a month free but shook his hand and finalized the deal.

∽

There were so many doors with locks that the landlord gave me a drawstring bag filled with tagged keys.

The tow truck company had taken all the vehicles, but they left behind a mess. I hired day workers to clean the lot. The building needed lighting, but it was okay. From the street, only the empty lot was visible. It had nicely painted boards covering the fence that I planned to put signs on.

Elena and I walked through as it was being cleaned up. It was already looking much improved.

"You'll have to keep the gates to the lot open, or no one will see the building," Elena said.

I kept coming back to the corner where the office used to be. It had windows on both streets.

"Baby, it's your call, but you should work on getting the shop open. Then, plan out the taco thing you want to do."

"Taco thing?"

"Well, you know."

MIKE HAD ALREADY BEEN through it once but met me at the new shop one morning. We walked through the office building and the cleaned-up lot. I pointed out where I thought everything needed to be outside. Then we went inside the building where the shop would be housed.

"This is a prize," he said.

"You're the only one that thinks so," I said.

"Let me run it," he said.

"I might do that, but if I do, it has to be on a different basis. For starters, you need to start making more than Two hundred twenty-five a week plus a few fringes that I've tossed your way."

Mike's grin was spectacular.

"About time," he said.

"Things are tight. I'm selling the insurance paper for twenty percent off the top, and I'm still not sure I'm making twenty percent on each job. There is also the possibility that Sam will realize how much he has tied up in paper and want to cool it."

"I get it," Mike said. "You got to be making twenty percent, but the bank is squeezing you."

"It's Sam, not the bank."

"I know, but for you, he's a bank."

I shrugged in agreement.

"Adjusters we are doing business with and the two carriers who have us as a one-stop-shop at Brooklyn and Rowan will love this place. I believe they will send business here for their insureds closer to this shop than the other. I'm going to buy loan cars, probably six to start, and then I have to insure the cars. I could go on."

"Okay," Mike said. "Go on."

"Here's the deal. If you run this, Donald will do the accounting. He will come over and write the checks. You got to mail them out because I am not messing up my credit. If you don't have the money in the bank, you gotta float it like I do and cover it."

"I got three check cashing places we never used," he said. "You told me to find them, and I got them. I can do that. You know it ain't cheap."

"I know for sure it's not cheap."

"I know you know," Mike said, stretching out his hand for a handshake. "You hungry, man? How about we hit a taco stand or something?"

"There's a place I meet Sam," I said. "Good pastrami."

"My treat," Mike said.

So, we headed to Canter's Deli. It was for sure a good idea because I had a lot to tell Mike, and I was getting distracted by other things, like where I wanted to put the divisions, the equipment, the signs, the lights, the everything.

Eunice's long hair was piled up high on top of her head. I told her she looked very well, not to mention that her gray hair was now black. She was wearing a pair of thick black cat's eyeglasses.

She put us in the booth where Sam and I usually sat, brought us coffee, a coffee pot for the table, two towering pastramis, and left us alone.

"This shop is a new corporation," I told Mike. "I'm just waiting for the paperwork. The name of this shop is Whittier Auto Center. I will give you one-third of the business, providing you work like it's entirely yours. I will get the spray booth and oven. You make the payments. I will get the compressor, and you make the payments. You know what I go through with the other shops. I'll pay to fix it up. You need not worry about it, but you need to make sure everyone who works for this new corporation is paid."

"I can do that, brother." Mike always wanted to shake hands. If the conversation was long enough, I might have to shake his hand ten times. He had been like that at DVI. I had my hands on my sandwich, so that was one handshake deferred.

"I paid a year's worth of rent in advance. When I told you that, I wasn't kidding. I think that you should kick me back a third of what the monthly rent would have been. It's chump change if you make a go of it."

"No sweat, brother."

I put down my pastrami, and we shook hands. I filled my coffee cup, took a sip, and continued.

"I will do the improvements and not charge you back for it. If there is any maintenance to do, if the damn roof leaks or something, you have to take the money out of the Whittier shop's income and take care of it. Bottom line, I will give you the shop, turnkey. From there on, it's on you."

"I've got it, brother. I know the business now. I can handle this big fucker. I'm bored where I am. I'll need help with the front end."

"I'm thinking of Susie, but you'll be fucking her all the time and get nothing done."

"Not true. I know you're getting some from Susie."

"You know nothing," I said.

How would he know?

"I don't think you should hire anyone I need to train. I wish I could take Gil, but he's buried with Soto Street."

"I'll find someone, maybe Alexa. I don't need to have a live person at Whittier and Rowan. It's an advertising spot with signs and everything. It's always been a waste."

"Alexa would be good here. She knows the business, and she's smart. I've worked with her a couple of times you had her cover with me."

"How many times have you done it with Alexa?"

"Brother, I lost count. If it's important, I can figure it out." He grinned and took his last bite. He put his arm up, getting Eunice's attention, and he ordered a basket of pastries from the massive bakery case at the front of the store. He complimented Eunice on her glasses. I ordered a sandwich to go.

"Okay, go home and talk to Vicki. Make sure she's good with you working beyond punching a clock, like Elena and I do when we need to."

"Vicki is fine. She works all the time. I'll marry her ass if I end up making some money off this third you give me." He grinned, then laughed.

Eunice put the pastries on the table, collected our plates, gave me the Reuben I'd ordered for Elena, and brought a fresh pot of coffee.

I put a ten on the table. Mike put a ten on the table too, and grabbed the check. For once, I didn't argue.

"Think positive," I said.

"Hey, you won big."

"Hey, I took care of you, didn't I?"

"You did, brother. That three g's is a lot of bread for me. Thanks. I only wish I could go up with you to Vegas."

"Mike, I'm crazy going up there and risking it like I do. I can't afford to have two of us."

"Wrong. If I lose, you can win, and the other way around."

He had told me that before.

"I'm not planning to go anymore," I said. "I'm due to lose."

I had resisted the pastries to that point, but Mike pushed the basket in my direction. I took one of the smaller ones, triangular and flakey. It was full of apples and cream cheese. I'd have to run for an extra thirty minutes tomorrow morning, but it was worth it.

"No, don't talk like that."

"Mike, I don't want to discuss gambling. I don't want you cashing any checks from this place and running up to Vegas. Got it?" He had to know how I'd feel about his doing that, but it didn't hurt to say it aloud.

"Brother, I'd never do that."

We got up from the table and shook hands.

AT HOME that night with Elena, Mike became the topic of our after-dinner conversation. We were already in bed with the light off. The Tonight Show was on. Jack Paar had retired, and the new guy, Johnny Carson, was okay. His partner Ed reminded me a whole lot of Mike.

"You made him a partner?"

"Yes and no. It's not the greatest deal in the world for him. I gave him a number of conditions. Look, it's Mike. I haven't done anything for him, and we were tight at DVI. I gave him a job, but his fiancée Vicki is the one who really looked out for him. She's been taking care of him ever since they met on the bus when he got out of DVI."

"You gave him a job, gave him money to rent an apartment, bought him his car, gave him a bunch of clothes, and three thousand from your Vegas win. You do take care of him."

"Baby, the car is seven years old. I should have signed for him at the bank and let him buy a new car."

"I only hope he's able to do all the things you told me he's got to do."

"If he doesn't, I'll close the shop, so help me. It's a different corporation. It's a standalone, and for a year, I don't have to mess with paying rent."

She sighed and took my hand. "You're so smart, baby."

"Don't tell me that. I'm not smart. I'm just filled with angles."

"When did you come up with paying him a year's rent in advance to get the rent down?"

"About an hour before I headed to meet him. That's why I took the cash."

"Were you really going to walk if he had not gone down on the rent?"

"I was halfway out the door when he relented. For sure, it was my last trip to see him if he didn't budge on rent."

"When you compare the size of the empty lot, the building with a roof, and the so-called Taquería-to-be, the property's bigger than the El Monte mortuary. The one on Brooklyn Avenue is bigger, though."

"So, what are you saying?" I asked.

With a straight face, she said, "It's big but not big enough for a good-sized mortuary."

I was puzzled. She broke out laughing.

"I'm *not* planning to open a mortuary," I said.

"Maybe you should, baby. Seems a lot less complicated."

It was my turn to laugh.

"I'm probably not going to own a mortuary. But someday, I'm going to own a whole bunch of property," I said.

She touched my face. I turned to look at her.

"I believe you," she said.

HOLMBERG SURPRISED me when he gave me the run around about financing the spray booth, oven, and compressor. No doubt he didn't want to help me dig my own grave, but I wasn't happy about it. He knew I had paid the rent for a year, making it difficult to finance the basic equipment I needed. At the time, I owed his bank less than twenty thousand on the equipment he financed for the Soto Street and Car Wash shops.

I went to Kitty. She gave me the equipment loan with the condition that I front one-third of the cost, a condition Holmberg never made. I took her up on it. I still had the ten thousand line of credit that I had not used.

I delivered a beautiful business to Mike, and it was on a street that had as much or more traffic as my first shop, the cash cow of my operation. I took some of the insurance work from the shop I operated and sent it with the bodymen to work at Mike's place.

I made a new deal with Sam that he would continue to buy insurance work paper only after the job was completed at a cost of eighteen percent instead of twenty. Elena and I went on a hunt to promote Mike's shop with insurance companies to get more business.

Everyone had told me to get rid of insurance work, but now it was the lifeline. Sam was the fix. Don said that eighteen percent was expensive but necessary if I was going to do that kind of work. Kitty may have been my friend, but she was better friends with Sam for sure. She told me that eighteen percent was a great deal for me and that Sam was committing more money to buy receivables than she had ever seen him do with any other shop owner.

"He thinks the world of you, and so do I."

ABOUT THE AUTHOR

George Hatcher is a man who has always believed that the world is full of opportunities waiting for those bold enough to seize them. With a ninth-grade education and a wealth of unique experiences, he has faced the ups and downs of life head-on. At the age of 20, while serving time, George took the initiative to complete the assignments and tests necessary to earn his high school diploma. His own life is a treasure trove of stories waiting to be uncovered.

Over the years, George has enjoyed a diverse career as an entrepreneur, consultant, and strategist. He has served as a peacemaker for athletes and their parents, as well as a crisis management advisor for physicians and attorneys, achieving considerable success in client development and public relations. He is a licensed boxing manager in California, though he currently has no boxers signed.

George has logged over 200,000 air miles annually through business travel and pleasure trips with his wife. However, since the onset of COVID-19 in 2020, his travel has come to a halt. Now, in retirement, George finds that life remains an ongoing adventure. Unfortunately, he is fighting several new battles that he never anticipated, yet he continues to discover something new with each step.

As a passionate storyteller, George has published a dozen books and finds immense joy in writing. With the world opening up again, he has seized the opportunity to immerse himself fully in his literary pursuits. He currently resides in Rancho Mirage, California, with his wife, Molly, his partner for 59 years, and their home is filled with three cats and two macaws. Each experience in his life has taught him invaluable lessons about adaptability, perseverance, and a touch of luck. Like the person who hits their head just to feel the pleasure of stopping, George has made his share of mistakes—some more than once. He hopes others can learn from them as he has.

Now devoted entirely to writing, George Hatcher invites others to join him on this remarkable journey, filled with lessons and stories that showcase the beauty of life's unpredictability.

A longer bio is on his website at http://georgehatcher.com/bio/bio.html

www.ingramcontent.com/pod-product-compliance
Lightning Source LLC
Chambersburg PA
CBHW050526100526
44581CB00008B/145/J